To Jan

Much appreciation
for your interest. Best
wishes,

Evelyn Wolfson
April 1984

AMERICAN INDIAN UTENSILS

AMERICAN INDIAN UTENSILS

Make Your Own
Baskets, Pottery, and Woodenware
with Natural Materials

Evelyn Wolfson

Drawings and diagrams by Nancy Poydar

David McKay Company, Inc.
New York

Thanks most of all to Bill, Bennett, Dacia, Jason, Jonathan, and Amy. Thanks also to Dr. Jeffrey Brain, Curator, Peabody Museum, Harvard University; and to Dr. Willard Spence, Biology Department, Framingham State College, for reading and critiquing; to Helga Volkema for helping to gather materials; to Rita Anderson for weaving; to Torj Wray for potting; to Ginny Steel for carving; to Nancy Lewis for photographs; and to Diane Frederickson, Dorothy Dundon, and Carol Kassabian for typing.

Library of Congress Cataloging in Publication Data

Wolfson, Evelyn.
  American Indian utensils.

  Bibliography: p
  Includes index.
  1. Indian craft. 2. Nature craft. I. Title.
TT22.W64   745.5   79-2112
ISBN 0-679-20505-5

  2 3 4 5 6 7 8 9 10

Manufactured in the United States of America

To Nancy

CONTENTS

INTRODUCTION

North America was once a vast wilderness. The coastal areas, plains, basins, deserts, prairies and forested mountain regions were rich in plant and animal life. Fish spawned in clear mountain streams; snow-capped peaks brought late summers with fresh crops of berries and nuts. Each of North America's varied environments had its own kinds of resources.

The first inhabitants of North America were hunters, fishermen and wild-food gatherers. They did not have permanent homes, but moved constantly in search of food. Plants were probably the easiest food to obtain because they did not require special tools. The hands, a large stone, and a stick were adequate for gathering and preparing seeds, roots, and greens which could be eaten raw. Fish were caught by hand or in crude traps concocted of stones and sticks. Only hunting required special tools. For thousands of years, Native American tribes made and used stone, bone, and shell spears and scrapers of all shapes and sizes. Many of these tools have been unearthed throughout the continent.

The Indians of North America eventually established permanent settlements in which they developed their own unique lifestyles. In order to take advantage of the plants and animals of the region, they had to create special tools and utensils. Tribes that gathered foods the year round, or remained nomadic, needed lightweight containers for gathering, transporting, and storing their foods. Baskets had to be woven tightly enough to hold water. Cooking in baskets, or stone-boiling, was accomplished by adding hot stones from a fire to a basket containing water, meat, and vegetables. In California, the plateau region, and the Northwest, the craft of basketry was highly developed. The tribes in these regions had a wide variety of natural materials with which to weave. Because stone grinders and other utensils were too heavy and cumbersome for travel by foot, they were buried where they were used and uncovered when needed. Only the Northwestern tribes were able to carry heavy wooden boxes on seasonal moves because travel in that region was by canoe. Natural materials in the Northwest favored woodworking, and the tribes in that area developed wooden utensils unique to the region. When Indians in the Great Plains acquired horses that had escaped from the Spanish explorers, many of the men became buffalo hunters. Buffalo horns and bones supplied them with materials for most of their tools and utensils. Thus, only a few baskets, pots, or wooden utensils were produced in the Plains region.

In the Great Basin, where skill and ingenuity were needed to collect enough food to stay alive, tightly woven containers were created to carry precious supplies of water and to hold tiny desert seeds.

In the Southwest, utensils were woven with desert grass and

shrubs long before agriculture became established. The more settled life-style created by farming allowed tribes to fashion utensils out of the rich clay soils of the desert. Woven utensils, used for cooking and for carrying and storing water, were replaced by pottery, which was more efficient and durable and easier to make.

Tribes of the Southeast, who made baskets and pots before they adopted farming, created many utensils out of wood. In the Northeast, basketry was an early craft; pottery making increased when tribes of the region took up farming. They also made special utensils out of wood and bark. For example, in the Great Lakes region, where white birch and maple trees abounded, tribes fashioned containers out of birch bark to collect their annual supply of maple sap. Always adaptive and inventive, Native Americans replaced their handmade utensils with brass, iron, and china when these materials later became available.

Today we are in awe of the beauty and workmanship of many ancient baskets, pots, and woodenware created with only the materials of nature, a pair of hands, and a few tools. Some North American Indians have recently revived traditional crafts, and they are now art forms. Baskets, pottery, and woodenware command high prices and are eagerly sought by collectors.

While it takes a great deal of experience to re-create the preparation of many of the natural materials once used by Native Americans and to duplicate techniques, much satisfaction can be gained by experimenting with the materials in our environment today. It is fun to identify, collect, and prepare natural materials. Six easy-to-work, common plants, used by tribes of North America, are included in this book. You will also find suggestions for locating natural clay deposits. After you have made just one utensil out of a natural material, you will develop a lasting awareness of the potential of the plants and soils around you.

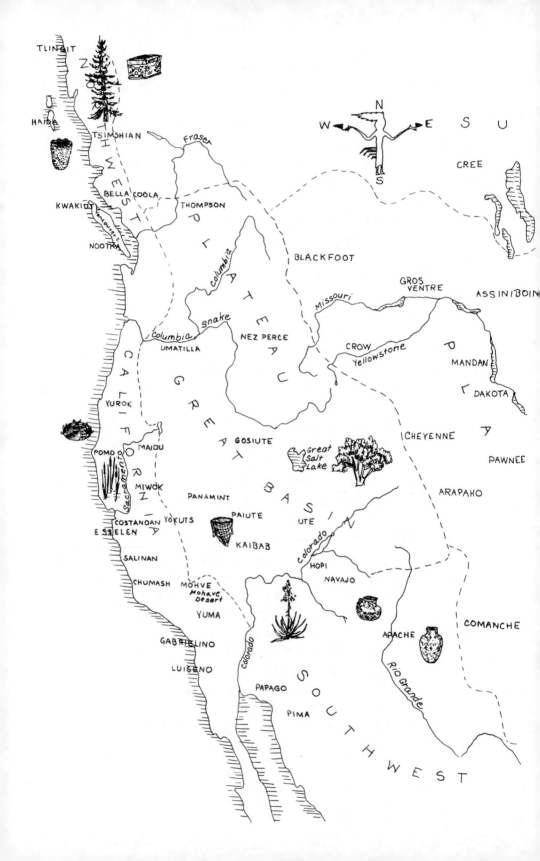

Map includes regional distribution of typical household utensils and natural materials for eight cultural areas of the North American Indians.

MAJOR TRIBES OF NORTH AMERICA

California-Northwest

Bella Bella
Bella Coola
Chinook
Chumash
Costanoan
Esselen
Gabrielino
Haida
Hupa
Karok
Klamath
Kwakiutl

Luiseño
Maidu
Miwok
Modoc
Mohave
Nootka
Pomo
Quinault
Salish
Salinan
Tlingit
Tsimshian
Wintun
Yokut

Yuma
Yurok

Great Basin-Plateau

Bannock
Cayuse
Flathead
Goshute
Kaibab
Nez Percé
Paiute
Panamint
Shoshone

Shuswap
Thompson
Umatilla
Ute
Washo
Yakima

Southwest

Acoma
Apache
Havasupai
Hopi
Jemez
Jicarilla
Maricopa
Navajo
Papago
Pima
Pueblo
Walapai
Zuñi

Plains

Arapaho
Arikara
Assiniboin
Blackfoot
Cheyenne
Comanche
Crow
Dakota
Gros Ventre
Iowa
Kansa
Kiowa

Mandan
Missouri
Osage
Oto
Pawnee
Quapaw
Santee
Sioux
Wichita
Yanktonnai

Southeast

Apalachee
Atakapa
Caddo
Catawba
Cherokee
Chickasaw
Chitimacha
Choctaw
Creek
Natchez
Pensacola
Powhatan
Seminole
Timucua
Tamathli
Tuscarora
Yuchi

Northeast

Abnaki
Algonkian
Beothuk
Cayuga

Chippewa
Delaware
Erie
Fox
Huron
Illinois
Iroquois
Kickapoo
Malecite
Massachusetts
Menomini
Miami
Micmac
Mohawk
Mohican
Montauk
Narragansett
Neutral
Ojibwa
Oneida
Onondaga
Ottawa
Passamaquoddy
Pennacook
Penobscot
Peoria
Pequot
Piankashaw
Potawatomi
Prairie
Sauk
Shawnee
Seneca
Susquehanna
Wampanoag
Winnebago

Map of basket regions.

Group baskets.

1

BASKETRY

Techniques

Native American baskets and mats involved three basic techniques: twining, coiling, and plaiting. Each culture area of North America used the technique best suited for the materials and life-style of the region. Baskets and mats were woven in a variety of shapes and sizes using variations of the basic techniques. Like textile weaving, basketry involves a warp and weft. The warp of a basket is the material used to form the frame or length of the basket; the weft is the material that is worked back and forth across the warp. Twining is done by twisting a pair of weft elements around a vertical warp. In

Twining
technique.

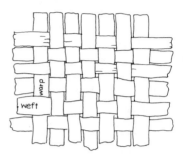
Plaiting technique.

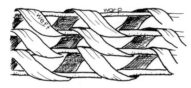
Coiling technique.

coiling, the warp is the horizontal group of fibers and the weft is the flexible fiber used to sew the warp pieces together. In plaiting, both the warp and weft elements are the same size and shape and have equal flexibility or rigidity. Most tribes used all techniques, although regional materials often suited one particular technique. A technique used to make baskets and mats often gives a clue to the region in which they were made. The plaited oak or cane baskets of the Northeast and Southeast, for example, are very different from the tightly twined and coiled baskets of the California or Northwestern Indians. Needless to say, a mat twined with rushes has a very different appearance than a mat plaited with cane.

Northwest

Trees in the Pacific Northwest grow to great heights. Dense evergreen growth is encouraged by the mild, year-round temperatures. Also, warm coastal currents, coming in contact with cool coastal mountains, create vapor that permeates the air in the form of fog, mist, and rain. Conifer trees do not sink deep roots, but spread long, horizontal roots close to the

2

surface. With so much moisture in the environment, the tough conifer roots grow quite long. Northwest Coast Indians were so proficient at gathering, preparing, and weaving these roots that the art of basketry rivaled woodworking throughout most of this region.

Life focused on fishing, and lightweight household utensils were essential for traveling with the migrating fish. In spring, when the fish began spawning, the tribes left their winter plank houses, packed their belongings in tall, cylindrical baskets, and traveled to their favorite fishing sites. It was the men's job to carve wooden household utensils and to weave the fishing nets. Dip nets of plant and bark fibers were made of two-inch-wide mesh netting. They were tied to a strong rim of yew wood attached to a long handle. The dip nets were dropped, with the opening in the direction of migrating fish, into rapidly running water.

While the men fished, the women dug long cedar and spruce roots for weaving with pointed sticks. The best roots were taken from mature trees two feet in diameter. The roots had to be pliable, of uniform size, and free of knots or shoots. A young spruce less than a foot in diameter provided only fair roots. However, these were often used because they were easy to take from the ground. Root bark was removed with knives made of medium-sized, sharpened mussel shells. The roots were bundled and stored for winter, when they were split,

Tlingit basket made of coiled spruce roots.

soaked, and woven into baskets. Conifer roots lend themselves to the technique of twining—the favored method of Northwest Coast tribes. However, rushes, cattail, cedar bark, and shrubs were also used to coil and plait baskets and mats.

Shellfish were gathered along the coast in openwork baskets, carried on the back. Indian women dug and smoked large quantities of clams, which they strung on cedar-string lines. The clams were stored in open baskets that allowed air to circulate. The clam strings were used for trade with the Cowlitz and Klickitat, two inland tribes who made coiled cooking baskets.

In fall, small groups of women picked berries in the mountains. The smallest basket, which could hold about one quart of berries, hung from the neck to keep the hands free. When one basket was full, the berries were emptied into another basket. When that basket was full, its contents were emptied into a larger basket on the ground. Because the richly decorated baskets became stained with berry juice, they were washed in fast-running water as soon as they were emptied. Some of these baskets were so soft and flexible they could be folded up and stored in a wooden box for the following year.

Berries and fish were boiled in tightly woven bucket-shaped baskets containing water and hot rocks. Shallow, openwork strainers were used to remove the food from the cooking basket. Fish, roasted on sticks in front of the fire, was served on mats woven of cedar bark, cattails, or rushes. Children ate out of shallow, twined dishes with flared sides. Water was passed around after the meal in a tightly-woven water vessel. A cedar-bark napkin was also passed around at the end of the meal. Cedar-bark mats, plaited of long, narrow strips of bark, were soft but tough. They could be washed repeatedly in running water. When cedar bark was not available, cattails and sedges were used for weaving. The Tsimshian, Kwakiutl, Nootka, and Bellacoola tribes made plaited cedar-bark mats and baskets.

California

A narrow coastal plain extends along the Pacific Coast, from the Mexican border to Oregon. Numerous mountain chains, with broken ridges and spurs, extend along the coast. Redwood and pine forests predominate in the northern area, while fertile, grassy valleys fill the coastal spurs and areas inland. There are flowing mountain rivers and streams, fringed with willows, alders, tules, and cattails. Indians of the region lived off the land all year round. They gathered fruits, berries, and greens in season, and they hunted and fished. In addition to an abundant supply of food, the variety of plants suitable for weaving enabled California tribes to be some of the most skillful basketmakers in North America. Woven household utensils were used for collecting foods, cooking, and water storage.

Many California tribes depended on the acorn crops for their food, and they wove special baskets for carrying, cooking, and storing acorns. A deep, cone-shaped basket was used for collecting them. When full, the basket was carried in a hammock, supported around the forehead with a tumpline. Acorns were sun-dried until the nutmeat could be easily picked from the shell with a fine bone. Then the meat was stored in large, tightly woven baskets. Only enough nutmeat for one meal was removed from storage and pounded into flour on a round, indented stone. The grinding stone was covered with a bottomless basket with flaring sides that served as a mortar. The basket bottom was cemented to the stone with pine pitch. The pitch was heated until soft, then placed around the base of the basket and set on the stone. When the pitch cooled, it became quite hard. A shallow basket, called a *dela,* was placed beside the mortar to collect the acorn flour as it was ground. The flour was washed as many as ten times, to remove tannin.

5

Poma woman grinding acorns with a stone pestle in a basket mortar. *(Smithsonian Institution National Anthropological Archives)*

Tolowa basketmaker. *(Smithsonian Institution National Anthropological Archives)*

Only a very few California tribes made clay vessels for cooking. The majority of the Indians boiled their foods in baskets containing water and hot stones. Acorn mush was made by adding acorn flour to a basket of boiling water. It was done when it reached the consistency of oatmeal. When cool, the mush hardened and was sliced and eaten by hand.

In the north, the Hupa, Karock, and Yurok collected and prepared conifer and alder roots for weaving. Further south, the Klamath and Modoc tribes made beautifully twined baskets out of tule root—a grasslike plant that spreads long, tough horizontal roots in wet, miry soils. Tule roots were dug in the spring with a three-pronged wooden fork. The roots had to be untangled gently so that they would not break. Because gathering the roots took a great deal of time and patience, families returned to the same spot each year to keep the tules pruned. After the roots were dug, the bark was immediately scraped off, and the roots were split down the middle. Bundles of roots were coiled and dried for about six months. When ready for use, they were soaked in hot water for about half an hour, and were kept moist while being woven. Tule roots were often dyed by boiling them in water to which walnuts and rusty metal had been added.

The Pomo Indians of central California were some of the region's most skillful basketmakers. They twined and coiled handsome baskets out of willow, redbud, and tule. Pomo baskets often had as many as sixty stitches to the inch. The tribe also decorated their baskets with feathers and shells. Sometimes, a finely coiled basket was covered with the scarlet scalp feathers of as many as twenty woodpeckers. One of the finest tributes a woman could make to dead relatives or friends was to bury them with a basket that took months to weave.

The Yokuts made use of the same materials as the Pomo, and they specialized in broad-bodied, flat-shouldered baskets, with narrow necks. Both the Yokuts and their neighbors, the Mono, coiled a wide variety of baskets.

Great Basin–Plateau

Indians of the Great Basin had few natural materials with which to work because cold, dry winters and hot, dry summers create a semidesert environment in which few plants survive. Those that do, adapt to the extreme temperatures and long periods of drought. Desert shrub and bare salt flats characterize large portions of the Great Basin. Sagebrush, desert grass, and broad-leaved herbs predominate in the very central portion. There are virtually no trees in the region. Mountains that crisscross the Basin are too low or too isolated to catch moisture from prevailing westerly winds.

Great Basin tribes traveled long distances from the low valleys to the mountains, collecting wild foods and gathering weaving materials. Baskets were woven of willow and osier shrubs that grew along canyon creeks and seasonal water holes. The shrubs were used in combination with desert sage and tough desert grasses. Willow shrubs were cut in spring and fall. Only long, straight shoots, with buds spaced far apart, were chosen. Bark was removed immediately after cutting because it stripped off very easily when fresh. Shoots were made even by scraping with a sharp stone, then they were tied in bundles to dry. Utensils for storing water, cooking, and seed-gathering were so important to Indians of the Great Basin that basketry became their chief craft. Water baskets were tightly coiled, with flat or round bottoms, flared sides, and narrow necks. They had small wood or horsehair loops on one side to which a woven or rawhide band was attached. The band fitted over the forehead, supporting the basket on the person's back. Baskets were made waterproof by dropping inside small, round stones that had been dipped in hot piñon pine pitch. The stones were shaken around until the pitch adhered to the inside of the basket. Though there is ample clay for pottery making in the region, only a few clay vessels

Paiute woman making baskets. *(Smithsonian Institution National Anthropological Archives)*

have been unearthed. Heavy, fragile pottery containers were not practical for the nomadic life-styles of the Great Basin tribes.

In summer and fall, they gathered small seeds from wild flowers and grasses. Some of the seeds were so tiny that the baskets for collecting and roasting them had to be very tightly woven. Ute women gathered seeds in large funnel-shaped baskets. The seeds were beaten into the basket with a fan-shaped beater. When the baskets were full, they were usually carried on the back by a strap that went around the lower portion of the basket to the forehead. In fall, the men gathered seeds from piñon pine trees. They pulled piñon cones off the tree with a hook tied to a long pole. The cones were first placed on mats or large, openwork baskets. They were then dried in the sun or were roasted all night under a cover of earth and branches until the tiny seeds which grow under the scales of the cones came loose. Surplus seeds were stored in pits dug in the ground and lined with animal skins. Piñon pine seeds were roasted in tightly coiled, shallow baskets made of grass and flexible twigs, to which round, hot stones were added. The stones were shaken around to keep them from burning the bottom of the baskets and to roast evenly. When fully roasted, the seeds were ground into fine powder on a flat rock.

Water was more plentiful in the plateau region north of the Great Basin. Forested valleys and grassy areas provided ample quantities of good weaving materials for Indians of the region. The Nez Percé Indians, as well as the tribes of southeastern Washington, preferred fibers from the stems of Indian hemp for weaving. Indian hemp has soft, flexible tissues on the inner bark of the stock that are very tough. The hemp, which reaches a height of five feet in damp areas, was gathered in the fall. After the leaves are gone, the stem fibers become reddish-brown. Hemp was prepared for weaving by splitting the stems down the centers to open them up. After they were folded in half, and peeled from the middle outward, the fibers were scraped with a sharp tool to soften them. Then they were twisted between the palm and thigh into long strands. If the hemp crop was overharvested, the bark of willow, chokecherry, antelope brush, sagebrush, and greasewood were used. Nez Percé tribes specialized in tightly twined bags, called "corn-husk bags." The name is deceptive, however, since the original bags were woven of hemp and decorated with squaw or bear grass that was gathered in late summer. Rare grasses for decoration were collected in the Bitterroot Mountains by Indian women traveling the Holu Trail. It was not until the introduction of corn to the region that grass overlay material was replaced by the inner leaves of corn husks, which are silky and quite pliable. This decorating technique is called "false embroidery," and is accomplished by wrapping a piece of dyed

Nez Percé
corn-husk
wallet.
*(Idaho
Historical
Society)*

Exhibition
of Nez Percé
handwork.
*(Idaho
Historical
Society)*

grass or corn husk around the *outside only* of the weft as it crosses the warp. In addition to corn-husk bags, the Indians of the plateau regions made large coiled oval utility baskets to gather camas bulbs and berries in season.

Southwest

The sparse vegetation of the desert Southwest did not hinder basket production for the Indians of the region. In fact, the earliest Pueblo Indians are referred to as "the Basketmakers." When the Spanish explorers came to the Southwest in the sixteenth century, Indians of the region were coaxing crops out of the parched desert soils. With the same patience and tenacity it took to farm, they also turned yucca and devil's claw—two tough desert plants—into finely woven utensils for everyday use. In addition, they scoured canyon creeks and seasonal water holes for weaving supplies of willow and cattail.

The leaves of most desert plants are very thin spines that prevent them from drying out. Yucca, however, is characterized by stiff, evergreen leaves crowded on a thick trunk. Yucca was an important plant for Indians of the Southwest, who used the leaves for weaving and also ate the buds, flowers, and flower stalks in season. Yucca leaves have multicelled fibers, extending through the pulpy tissue of the leaf stem, that can be stripped and made into strong cordage. In addition, the leaf itself can be cut into strips, dried, and plaited into baskets and mats.

Tribes of the Southwest were farmers who raised large crops of corn and beans and wove utensils for collecting and storing their crops. The Hopi carried harvested crops on their backs in large, wicker baskets, or in hammocks hung from the forehead. Woven hammocks and plaited headrings were made to hold pottery jars full of water. Corn was winnowed in shallow, rimless trays. Flat trays, made with coiled grass and yucca,

A Hopi carrying corn in a hammock. *(Eastern Washington State Historical Society)*

Pima woman with a burden basket. *(Smithsonian Institution National Anthropological Archives)*

were used for eating and for ceremonial purposes. Some of the finest coiled baskets attributed to the Hopi, particularly their wedding baskets, were actually traded from the Apache, Pima, and Paiute.

The Pima of Arizona, often called the "bean people," cultivated large crops of beans that survived better than corn in the hot desert climate. Accomplished basketmakers, the Pima still coil beautiful baskets out of cattail and willow. Their neighbors, the Papago, coiled most of their utensils out of bear grass—a smaller species of yucca—and out of devil's claw, a desert weed with hard seedpods. Two inner hooks, connected to each seedpod of devil's claw, yield a black material for weaving designs in baskets. The Papago had to trade with the Pima for weaving supplies of willow. In addition to gardening, the Papago harvested and prepared saguaro cactus fruit, which required specially woven utensils. The gathered fruit was carried on the head in shallow, coiled baskets. When cooked, the saguaro juice was strained and boiled into syrup. Seeds were removed by hand from the pulp and ground into oil and flour. Both the Pima and Papago made lace burden baskets, framed with devil's claws, and supported by poles of cactus wood.

The Jicarilla Indians of northern New Mexico coiled thick, household baskets for winnowing grain, parching corn, and boiling food. These containers were made of split willow or cottonwood twigs, and were characterized by looped handles of devil's claw. The Mescalero tribes, also of New Mexico, used the young shoots of squawberry and sumac to weave tall, flared-neck water jars, which were carried by tumplines around the chests. The Mescalero also coiled broad, flat baskets of yucca.

Papago woman weaving baskets. *(Smithsonian Institution National Anthropological Archives)*

Southeast

Much of the Southeast once consisted of woodlands of oak, pine, and tall cypresses, interspersed with grassy meadows and swamps. Tribes of the area used many different types of plants to create utensils for farming, fishing, and collecting wild foods.

Along the Gulf Coast, palmetto trees flourish. The palmetto is a palm tree characterized by broad, fan-shaped leaves. Indians of the region, who used the large leaves of these trees

15

to thatch their homes, also made cord from the tough fibers along the leafstalks. Coastal tribes, who spent a great deal of time fishing, created woven weirs by driving stakes into the shore and interweaving them with cane. Fish were dried on racks called "hurdles," made by weaving cane across horizontal frames, set on four posts near fires.

Cane was particularly abundant inland, where canebreaks grew in the rich, loamy soils bordering rivers and streams. Canebreaks are thickets of hollow-stemmed plants, usually bamboo, that grow as tall as trees. Over many years, floods caused the rivers of the Southeast to back up over the land, depositing soil along the banks. The larger soil particles, which settled first, were rich in nutrients and drained exceedingly well. The smaller soil particles, which settled last, were so fine that the water could not drain. This created swamps. Along some parts of the Mississippi River, these soil deposits, called "levee ridges," are three miles wide and twenty-five feet high. The soils in which cane flourished were well suited for crops, and Indians of the region planted small, but productive, gardens in these fertile strips of land. River cane lends itself well to plaiting—a weaving technique that requires the same warp and weft. It was commonly used by the Cherokee, the Oklahoma, the Chitimacha, and the Choctaw tribes. Cane was also used to build houses and fashion tools for weaving. The plant is hollow inside, and has a hard, brittle outer stem that can be easily split into splints of uniform width. The splints were trimmed, scraped, and often dyed before they were woven into baskets and mats. Butternuts, black walnuts, and bloodroot were used for dyes. By alternating dyed with natural splints to create checkerwork or twilled patterns, the tribes of the Southeast created beautiful baskets and mats.

Many woven utensils were used to prepare, carry, and store corn. Corn sieves were made by spacing splints apart, depending on how large a mesh was needed. Tall cane burden baskets, with flared sides, were used by the Choctaw to carry

Mrs. Sweeney Willis is making cane
baskets with oak handles. *(U.S.
Department of the Interior, Indian
Arts and Crafts Board)*

Choctaw cane mat. *(U.S. Department of the Interior, Indian Arts
and Crafts Board)*

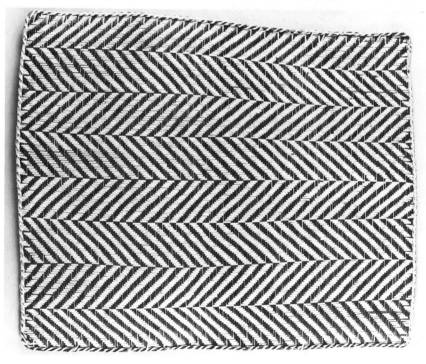

Lottie Stamper, Cherokee instructor, teaching oak-splint basketry. *(U.S. Department of the Interior, Indian Arts and Crafts)*

corn and heavy loads. Large, plaited cane mats were used for bedding, carpets, curtains, house coverings, and blankets in which to wrap the dead. The Cherokee, of northern Georgia and the Appalachian Mountains, made baskets out of both cane and oak splints.

Cane splints can be easily recognized by their shiny surfaces, while oak splints are dull in appearance. Open-bottom baskets for sifting ground meal were made of narrow oak splints. The Cherokee also made flared baskets and flat trays with shapes unique to the region.

Northeast

A scouting party of Pilgrims uncovered a large cache of Indian corn, stored in a tall basket with a narrow neck, in Wellfleet on Cape Cod. Similar broad, bottle-shaped baskets with corn cob stoppers were used by many tribes of the Northeast to store corn for the winter. These were important utensils for the tribes who were mainly farmers. Unfortunately, basketmaking did not last long after the arrival of European settlers, and the story of weaving in this region is not complete.

Most Northeastern tribes created baskets out of wood splints—thin strips of wood pounded from a cut log. The log was first soaked in water until the cells were filled. Then it was pounded firmly over its entire length. Pounding separated the cellular portion of each year's growth; the annual layers of wood separated into long, thin strips. The strips were peeled off, one at a time. They were then cut into narrow splints and sometimes dyed. Black ash was preferred by basketmakers because it was pliable when dry and less brittle than white ash or oak. Although hickory was considered durable, the wood was difficult to separate into annular layers. Maple split easily into the right thickness, but did not last well.

Wood splints probably evolved from the use of cane splints used in the Southeast. The splints were plaited into a variety of patterns: Checker weaving was created by a simple over-one and under-one procedure; twilled weaving—an under-two and over-two technique—combined dyed and natural splints to create beautiful designs; wicker weaving, also an over-one and under-one process, was used to make fish weirs and carrying baskets. Wicker burden baskets for harvesting corn were strapped on the back. Deep baskets with flexible sides and loosely woven bottoms were used for washing hulled corn. Shallow, hickory-splint sifting baskets were used to prepare cornmeal. Round and square berry-picking baskets were designed to be tied around the waist to free the hands. Shallow, rectangular baskets were used to dry berries in the sun.

The Oneida, one of the five tribes of the Iroquois, made attractive, black ash splint baskets with decorated borders. The decorations were often applied with a potato stamp. After a design had been cut out of the flat side of halved potato, it

Mohawk woman weaving a basket. *(Smithsonian Institution National Anthropological Archives)*

was dipped in a plant dye and pressed against the border splints at the top of a basket.

Because the Iroquois tribes were very skillful farmers, it is not surprising they made use of corn husks for weaving. Corn-husk baskets were made by coiling and sewing the husks or by braiding them into strips which were sewn together. Twined, watertight bottles, salt dishes, and mats were also made of corn husks. In addition, the Iroquois made very clever doormats, woven so that the husk ends protruded from one side and created a stiff pile to wipe muddy feet.

Tribes of the Great Lakes continued to make baskets until the twentieth century. Birch, beech, maple, basswood, and elm were used for simple wood-splint baskets. Cattails, rushes, and nettle, as well as the bark of basswood, white cedar, and slipper elm were used to twine bags. Coiled baskets were made of both plant fibers and sweet grass. Nettle, which grows abundantly in the region, was harvested in the fall, tied in bundles, and hung to dry. The woody outer stalk was stripped away to expose the fine inner fibers. The fibers were rolled against the thigh and twisted into cordage. These were then used in the making of strong bags, clothing, fishnets, and animal snares. Elm, red cedar, and basswood bark were stripped from trees in the spring, when the sap flows. The bark was torn into strips and soaked in a lake or stream. The bark was taken from the water when the inner bark peeled away from the outer bark and separated into fine fibers. These were used for fishlines and general household twines. Stronger fibers were made by boiling the inner bark and pulling the fibers back and forth through the shoulder or pelvic bone of a deer.

Twined bags were made by hanging warp fibers from a piece of twine wrapped horizontally around two posts set in the ground. Warp fibers were tied to the horizontal twine and hung vertically. Weft fibers were then woven from left to right across the warp. These bags were particularly useful for carrying household items.

Bulrush and cedar-bark mats and bags were made on the same type of loom. Bulrushes were suspended from a crossbar; basswood fibers were twined from left to right at about one-half-inch intervals. Cedar bark was woven in the same manner, using a simple over-and-under technique.

The traditional method of preparing cattail mats to cover a wigwam was done by sewing rather than weaving. Cattail leaves were cut evenly, lined up on a flat surface, and sewn with a long needle threaded with bark fiber. These mats were also used as floor coverings, room dividers, and food servers.

The art of sweet-grass basketry has long been a tradition among the Chippewa. This plant flourishes in the north, along the Atlantic Coast and in the meadows and prairies around the Great Lakes. It was used to coil round and oval bowls, trinket baskets, trays, and dishes. The Indians of the region also used sweetgrass to decorate splint and bark containers.

Chippewa woman weaving a rush mat. *(Smithsonian Institution National Anthropological Archives)*

Gathering cattail sedges.

Technique of sewing cattail mats.

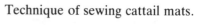

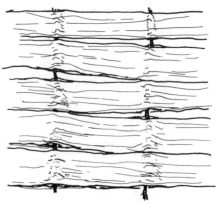

Plants for Weaving

BLACK WILLOW *(Salix nigra)*

At least a hundred species of willow grow throughout the United States and Canada. Black willow trees grow near water in all states east of the Rocky Mountains except the Dakotas. They reach a height of about 100 feet in the lower Mississippi Valley: a height of forty feet is typical in the rest of its range.

Black willow is broad-crowned, with crooked branches and a short trunk. The bark is blackish-brown, with deep, narrow cracks. Slender, fast-growing twigs can be identified by their brown-to-orange hues. Leaves are 3 to 6 inches long and about ¾ inch wide. They are light green, finely toothed, and shiny. Green flowers appear in the form of tassels with new spring leaves. Fruits are small, brown, catkins, each about ¼ inch

Black willow.

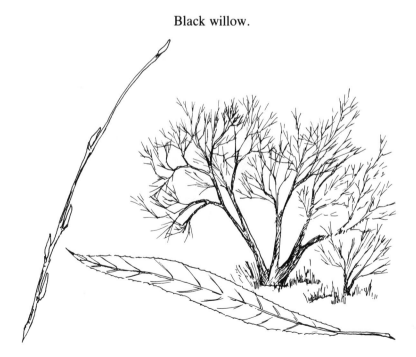

long. The tiny fruit seeds are covered with fine hairs that aid in the seeds' dispersal. The wood of black willow is probably the lightest weight of all the Eastern hardwoods. The sapwood is made up of springy fibers that give it great flexibility—the reason why willow was a popular weaving material among the tribes of North America.

Today, black willow trees are chiefly used to anchor soil along riverbanks and prevent erosion. Willow wood is also used for boxes, crates, waterwheels, boats, and wooden toys.

CATTAIL *(Typha latifolia* and *T. angustifolia)*

About ten species of cattail grow throughout the United States, along the banks of rivers, streams, and ponds, and in marshlands. Narrow-leaved cattail grows throughout the eastern half of the United States, along the Pacific Coast from southern Washington through southern California, and in

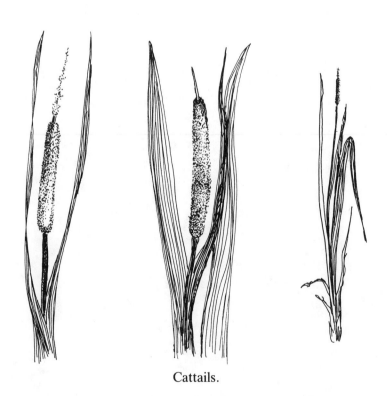

Cattails.

southwestern Arizona. Broad-leaved cattail grows in marsh-lands throughout North America and is commonly found inland.

Cattails, which grow to a height of six or more feet, are perennial herbs, which means the stout, horizontal rootstocks remain in the ground all year round. Growth begins in spring and terminates in fall. Their leaves are tall, flat, and green, and are filled with large air holes. Brown flower spikes grace the ends of the tall stalks in early summer. When they break during winter and early spring, they disperse tiny seeds.

Cattail leaves were harvested and dried in late summer by Native Americans. The dried leaves were well suited for weaving because they were tough and flexible. Indians of the Northeast sewed individual cattail leaves together with basswood cordage to make mats for covering their wigwams.

SPANISH BAYONET, YUCCA *(Yucca filamentosa)*

Spanish bayonet grows around the Gulf of Mexico, north to Virginia. Five other species of yucca that grace the deserts of the Southwest were harvested by Indians of the region.

Yucca.

Yucca is characterized by stiff, sword-shaped evergreen leaves, about 2½ feet long and 2½ inches wide. The bell-shaped flowers are white with purple tips. The mature fruit is a capsule of dry seeds. Pollination of yucca depends on a small species of moth. In the process of laying her eggs in the ovary of the yucca, the moth causes pollen to come in contact with the pistil, thus fertilizing the plant. Fortunately, yucca plants produce enough seeds to feed the moth larvae and to ensure their own future. Yucca plants could not survive, however, were it not for the little moth.

Tribes in the Southwest removed the yucca's tough fibers from the pulpy tissue of immature leaves to make twine. Split yucca leaves were used to weave baskets and mats. Some species of yucca yield a soapy juice that can be made to lather. This was used as a hair wash.

How to Make a Twined Basket

Materials

10   shoots, each 10 inches long and
     approximately ¼ inch in diameter
40   vines, 6 feet long and approximately ⅛
     inch in diameter
1   clam shell, penknife, or pair of scissors
   A shallow pan of water
   Hedge clippers

1. Soak all materials in warm water for at least 15 minutes. Keep the weaving materials wet as you work.

2. Line up five 10-inch shoots in your left hand and place the remaining five 10-inch shoots perpendicular to the

Starting weft around warp.

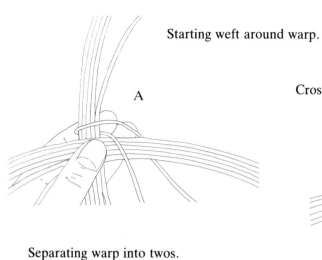

A

Crossing weft after wrapping warp.

B

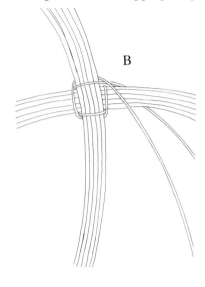

Separating warp into twos.

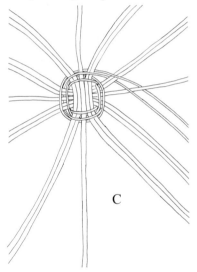

C

D

Separating warp into ones.

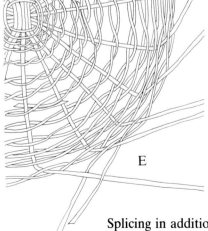

E

Splicing in additional pieces of weft.

first group under the left thumb *(A)*. This is the warp of the basket.

3. With the right hand, loop a 6-foot vine around the top of the first warp group. This long vine, the weft, will twine around the warp.

4. Cross the vine by bringing the bottom of the loop *over* and the top of the loop *under* the second warp group *(B)*. It is important that the weft cross at the end of each warp group.

5. Continue to loop in this manner twice around the warp.

6. Separate the warps into twos, ones, and twos, and twine around twice *(C)*.

Baskets twined with honeysuckle.

7. Separate the warps into ones, looping around each warp. Start the sides of the basket by gently pressing the warp upward and pulling the weft a little tighter each time around. Don't pull too tightly, otherwise the walls will turn inward. Continue to twine around each warp until the basket is finished. Keep dipping the warp into warm water to keep it pliable *(D)*.

8. Additional lengths of weft can be spliced, or added by placing a new weft along the one that is running out. Weave them together for half a turn *(E)*.

9. The open-weave basket with flared sides, as pictured, is a copy of an Indian berry-sifting basket. It was twined with honeysuckle vines in the warp and weft.

How to Make a Coiled Basket

Materials

> 4 pieces of twisted fiber, 6 to 8 inches long
> 6 bundles of sewing fiber, 18 inches long or longer (cattail, sedge, or grass)
> 1 large bundle of grass or vines
> 1 awl
> Shallow pan for water
> Pair of scissors (optional)

1. Soak all materials in warm water for 15 minutes. Remember to keep the materials wet as you work. Either dip your fingers in water to keep the sewing fiber wet, or dip the sewing fiber itself in water.

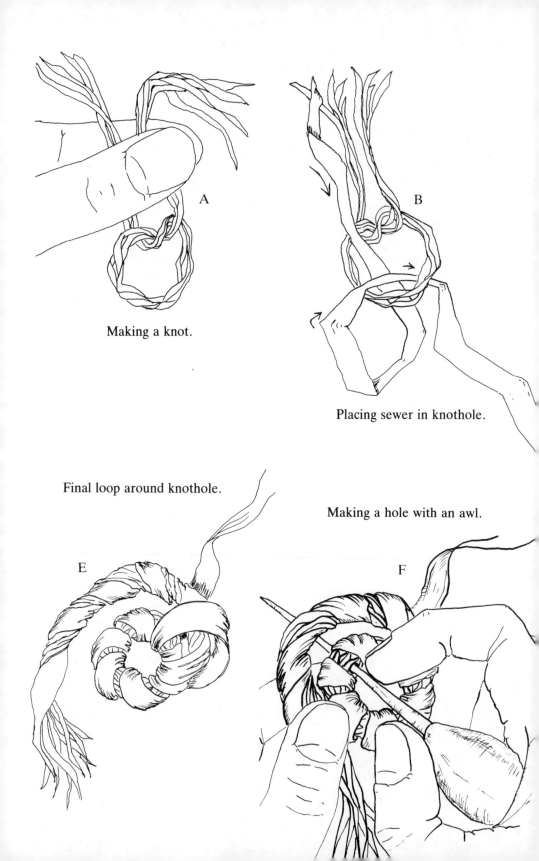

A

Making a knot.

B

Placing sewer in knothole.

Final loop around knothole.

Making a hole with an awl.

E

F

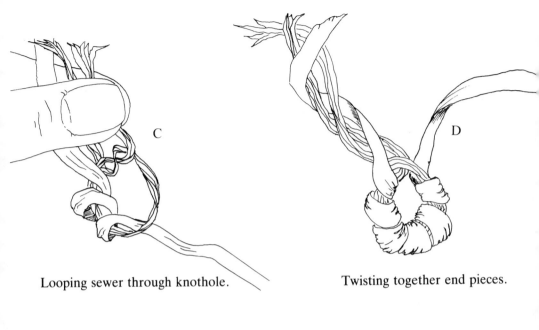

Looping sewer through knothole.

Twisting together end pieces.

Pulling sewer through a hole.

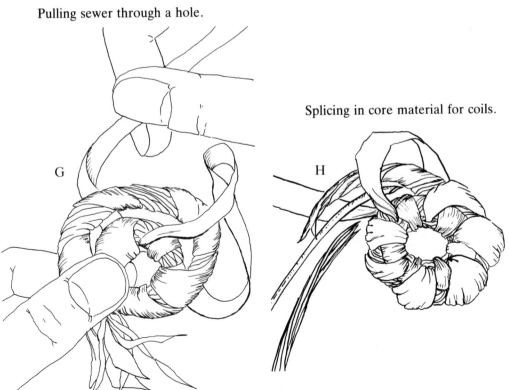

Splicing in core material for coils.

2. Make a loose knot in the center of the 4 short pieces of twisted fiber and bring the ends of the knot together in the left hand *(A)*.

3. Place one end of a sewing fiber alongside the knot ends, stick the other end down through the knot hole, and loop it around *(B)*.

4. Continue to loop the sewer around the knot *(C)*.

5. When the sewer has completely covered the fibers of the knothole, twist together tightly the end pieces in the left hand *(D)*.

6. Press the twisted fiber against the circle created by the knothole, and make one final loop around the

Coiled baskets made of cattail, sedge, honeysuckle, and pine needles.

knothole. This is the end of your first row *(E)*. Don't pull the sewing fiber too tightly because you will need to make an awl hole between "each" of the sewing stitches in the next row.

7. Using the awl, gently make a hole in the fibers of the first row *(F)*.

8. Insert the end of the sewing fiber in the awl hole and pull it through *(G)*.

9. Continue to make several more stitches in this manner. Be sure to introduce the material you plan to use for the core of your basket "before" the end fibers are completely wrapped *(H)*.

10. The baskets shown in the photograph are being worked with cattails, sedges, honeysuckle vines, and pine needles. These materials may be used in any combination.

How to Make a Plaited Mat

Materials

18-by-24	inch piece of fiberboard
2½-inch	wood strips
2	large elastic bands
20	reeds
	Pair of scissors
3	yards of natural fiber or household twine
	Penknife (optional)

33

1. Remove the leaves and split the reeds with your fingernail or a knife into narrow strips. Cut the strips into 18-inch lengths.

2. Nail two ½-inch strips of wood about 6 inches in from either end of the fiberboard.

3. Wrap elastic bands around the ½-inch wood strips and insert about 12 reeds under the elastic from one end to the other.

4. Take the additional reeds and weave them under and over in the other direction, perpendicular to the 12 reeds. These will be further apart than the first set of reeds lying lengthwise.

5. When you have woven in all the cross reeds, weave additional reeds lengthwise.

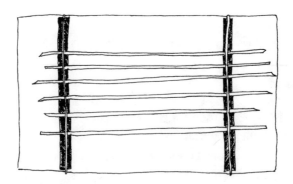

Placing reeds on a board for plaiting.

Weaving a plaited mat with reeds.

6. Continue to weave until you can no longer go under and over in either direction. Trim the edges all around with a pair of scissors.

7. Finish the ends by twining around each reed with a very soft piece of natural fiber or a piece of household twine. Wind it around the mat two or three times, or until you are sure the reeds are secure.

Map of pottery regions.

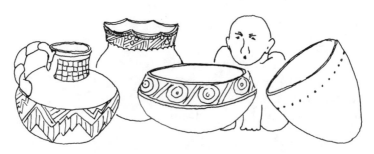

Group pots.

2

POTTERY

Techniques

In the regions of North America, where pottery making was a major industry, three basic techniques were used: coiling, modeling, and molding. Most pots were made by coiling, or by combining coiling and molding. Coiling is done by forming a ball of clay into a flat disk, and setting the disk in a shallow container. Additional clay balls are rolled out, one at a time, into coils that are placed on top of one another to form the walls of a vessel. Often, tools are used to shape and form coiled pots. One set of tools includes a paddle and an anvil. The paddle is smacked against the outside of the vessel, while the anvil—a rounded object made of pottery or stone—is used to support the inside wall. A simple gourd scraper is another tool used to shape the outside of a coiled vessel, while the fingers or a rounded stone is held inside.

Modeled pots are formed with the fingers by working a ball of clay into the required shape. Some modeled pots were enlarged by paddling the outside, while holding an anvil on the inside. Molding was done by placing a flat disk of clay inside a previously prepared container, such as a basket, a wooden bowl, or a pot, or by shaping a flat disk of clay over a prepared form.

Regardless of how a vessel was formed, it was usually decorated. To change the color of a pot, a slip was made by mixing water with any good-quality clay to the consistency of heavy cream, and applying it when the pot was "leather hard"—the stage when a pot is just stiff enough to be handled without changing its shape.

Southwest

When corn was introduced to the Indians of the Southwest, tribes of the region began to plant small gardens. The art of basketry, already well developed, had served the needs of an earlier nomadic life-style. Farming, however, created different household needs, and the Indians began experimenting with desert soils. In the desert, rainwater disappears quickly into porous soils or is turned away because there is no space for water to enter between the fine rock particles. Indians of the region developed methods to use the porous soils for their crops and the nonporous soils for irrigation ditches, adobe houses, and pottery making. At first, clay was mixed with sand. Clay utensils were probably originally used for cooking because they could be set directly over a fire. Eventually, jars were designed to carry water. Although they were not thoroughly waterproof, water could be carried in them for short distances.

Although pottery is fragile, potsherds, or pottery pieces, last for centuries. Fragments of polished red pottery, unearthed in caves and arid desert soils, indicate that pottery was being made in southwestern New Mexico and southeastern Arizona between A.D. 200 and A.D. 300. The potter's wheel was unknown to the Indians of North America. The tools,

Very rare Shoshoni pot. *(Idaho Historical Society)*

materials, and techniques that are used today in the Southwest are the same as those used almost 2000 years ago. Clay is still gathered, prepared, formed, decorated, and fired in traditional fashion. The coil-and-scrape technique was preferred by the Pueblo while the paddle-and-anvil method was practiced by tribes in the southern Arizona region.

Early Hohokam potters used the paddle-and-anvil technique to create large red-and-buff painted jars, bowls, and dishes. Farming tribes, who lived along the Salt and Gila rivers, and who may have been ancestors of the Hohokam, were skilled basketmakers but never developed an active potting industry. Their pottery includes only a few utilitarian

Prehistoric Hohokam vessel. *(Nancy Lewis)*

Prehistoric Pueblo bowl. *(Eastern Washington State Historical Society)*

vessels: crude water jars with flaring rims, bean pots, and parching trays.

The "Basketmakers," ancestors of the Pueblo, originally produced gray-colored, unpolished pots in the shape of baskets and gourds, decorated with simple designs. Later, they made corrugated pots by pressing together coil ridges. After many years, the Pueblo became skillful potters and created handsome coiled bowls, jars, and effigy mugs, painted with bold designs. The term *polychromatic,* meaning many colors, is often used to describe their work.

Early Pueblo villages were generally located some distance from cultivated fields. Carrying home the harvested crops and water was often a long and arduous task. Water, always scarce in the desert, was carried in tall, narrow-necked pottery jars, in a hammock slung on the back and supported around the forehead by a tumpline. Pueblo pottery, however, was not waterproof. Water, leaking from inside the vessel, formed tiny droplets on the outside and evaporated, which helped to keep the water inside cool. Too much evaporation made the jar impractical for long trips, so small ones were waterproofed with piñon pine pitch. Corn stew, a basic dish of the region, was cooked in a large pottery vessel set on a ring of stones over a fire. Corn was stored in clay pots and eaten from shallow clay bowls.

In northern Arizona, three mesas are still inhabited by the Hopi, ancestors of the earliest Pueblo tribes. The Hopi, who continue to make pottery, are known to be among some of the finest potters in the Southwest. Late in the nineteenth century, an archeologist hired a member of a Hopi clan to help with an archeological dig. The young Indian took pieces of the prehistoric pottery he found home to his wife, Nampeyo. She copied the designs on her pots and became a very famous potter.

Neighbors of the Hopi, the Zuñi, still live in the western portion of New Mexico. They produce large bowls and water jars with black-and-red designs on white backgrounds. South of Albuquerque, between the desert and the Rio Grande, Acoma pueblo sits on a high mesa, surrounded by rich deposits of various colored fine clays. Laguna and Islets pueblos nearby, share these clay sources, and all tribes create colorful pottery with red, orange, and black designs on white backgrounds. Further north, along the Rio Grande River, the pueblos of Cochiti, Santa Domingo, and San Felipe use the area's volcanic sand as temper that they mix with their clay. At Santa Ana and Zia pueblos, temper is gathered in the form of solid volcanic rock, which is then ground into sand. North of Santa Fé, potters from the pueblos of San Ildefonso, Santa Clara, and San Juan use fine-grained sand from the banks of the Rio Grande and Chuma rivers to temper a very fine local clay.

Early in the twentieth century, at San Ildefonso pueblo, Julian Martinez broke with local tradition and started to make pots with his wife Maria. Pottery making is traditionally a woman's responsibility. Together, they created beautiful, highly polished black and red pottery. They specialized in a

Santa Clara black pot.

Maria and Julian Martinez with their pots. *(Eastern Washington State Historical Society)*

firing technique called reduction, which means reducing the oxygen in the fire. This creates carbon, which turns the pots jet black. The Martinezes used finely pulverized animal dung to cover the fire at just the right time. Reduction firing was used with such success by the Martinezes that other Rio Grande pueblos were inspired to adopt the technique.

Many Indian women keep their clay source a secret, while others take their families on outings to dig clay. Many different clays can be found between the layers of desert sandstone. The clay becomes exposed where water repeatedly washes through the area. Women traditionally asked the earth's permission to dig the clay. Then an offering was often left at the site. A wooden digging stick was originally used to remove clay in chunks. These traditions are no longer practiced by all tribes, and the digging stick has been replaced by a shovel.

Large stones, sticks, and grass are taken out of the clay before it is put in carrying baskets. At home, it is ground like corn on a *metate,* a large indented stone, with a *mano,* or stone grinder. The clay is mixed with temper, if needed, and water. The women then knead clay until it "feels" right. A flat base of clay is placed in a support which allows the potter to rotate the pot as she works. Small bowls are made from one long coil, while larger vessels require a series of coils applied in stages. Coiled vessels are often covered with fine slips to provide smooth surfaces for polishing and painting. Slips are made by mixing any good-quality, untempered clay with water until it achieves the consistency of heavy cream. Slipped pots are either painted or polished with smooth, round polishing stones—highly prized family heirlooms, passed along from one generation to another. Many were collected along old riverbeds and streams, where they had been well tumbled over the ages. Early paintbrushes were made by chewing the end of a yucca leaf or by skinning a rabbit tail.

Paddle-and-anvil pots are generally made by building a coil

Hano Pueblo women making pots. *(Smithsonian Institution National Anthropological Archives)*

onto a clay base, formed over a convex mold. The coils are pressed on, then paddled downward with a wooden paddle. The pot is removed from the mold after all the coils are on and the clay is leather-hard.

Because wood in the Southwest is a precious commodity, dried animal dung (which burns slowly and evenly) and cedar bark are used as fuel. Pots are directly fired in shallow pits or directly on the ground. Native American pottery is low-fired because temperatures rarely get above 1700°F. in outdoor fires. The potters can tell by the red hue of the fire when the pots are done. Some Southwestern tribes did not allow talking while pots were being fired, fearing a voice would enter a pot and cause it to explode.

Southeast

Tribes of the Southeast were experimenting with the earth's minerals and producing pottery as early as 2500 B.C. The fertile valleys of the Mississippi River and its tributaries were excellent for farming, and large villages sprang up between present-day St. Louis, Missouri, and Natchez, Mississippi, during the Mississippi Period (A.D. 700–A.D. 1600). Pottery making was well developed by these farming tribes. Women made utensils of clay to store, prepare, and cook their harvested crops. This early pottery was polished and decorated with red slips, or designs cut into wet clay with sharp instruments. Designs were also created by pressing precut wood blocks into wet clay or by paddling the wet clay with a cord or fabric-wrapped paddle. During the Mississippi Period, tribes of the Southeast had a richly religious life for which ceremonial pots in the shapes of humans and other animals were made.

Along the lower Mississippi River, soils are well suited for farming, although there is frequent flooding and a lack of

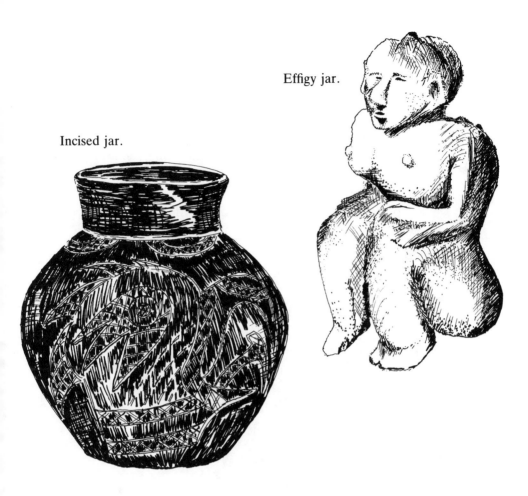

Effigy jar.

Incised jar.

minerals, like flint, for toolmaking. The Natchez Indians were living in the area along the lower Mississippi when European explorers arrived. Natchez pottery was decorated with plain or painted incised designs.

Much of the Southeast is a coastal plain, characterized by slow-moving rivers and vast swamps. The Apalachee and Timucua tribes of the area had small gardens, and abundant supplies of fish and shellfish. The Seminole, who migrated to Florida in the nineteenth century, were skillful potters who created a firing technique that produced polished black and cream pots. They brushed their pottery, when wet, with fiber bundles to create designs.

The Cherokee originally lived in the foothills and valleys of the southern Appalachian Mountains—a region rich in deposits of soapstone, which supplied the tribes with material to make their bowls and pots. Cherokee potters combined the techniques of molding and coiling, and their pottery was decorated with complex stamp designs. The Cherokee, Catawba, and Chitimacha of present-day Louisiana were also adept potters, and formed pots over gourds and other objects.

Cherokee women making pottery. *(Smithsonian Institution National Anthropological Archives)*

Traditional Native American pottery making was revived by the Catawba early in the twentieth century. Their pots were coiled, then wiped with a piece of wet material to remove excess clay and to fill in cracks. Polishing was done with a piece of bone or hard wood. Catawba decorating techniques included rubbing or rolling a corncob over the surface of the pot, or incising and impressing other objects into the clay. The pots were dried for several days before being fired. An old firing technique, called smudging, gave Catawba pottery a black finish. Smudging is very much like Southwestern reduction firing. After a fire reaches maximum temperature, it is smothered with oak bark to cut off oxygen and cause carbon buildup on the pots. A fire was made by piling oak bark around freshly made pots. Then a large, unfired vessel was placed on top of the pots, and the pots were covered with more bark. When the top bark was burning brightly, the bark underneath it was lit. Smoke backed up onto the pots, turning them jet black.

Southeastern tribes continued to make traditional pottery in the late eighteenth and early nineteenth centuries. Recent archeological evidence indicates that traditional crafts persisted after the tribes of the Southeast had been removed to Oklahoma.

Northeast

Corn was introduced into the Northeast during the Woodland Period, about A.D. 1000. Algonkian tribes established small settlements and planted vegetables gardens along the Atlantic coast and in the Connecticut River Valley. During this period, pottery making became an important industry. Tribes who quarried and worked soft talc, called steatite or soapstone, turned increasingly to pottery making. Algonkian tribes, living around the Great Lakes, had used birch-bark

Soapstone jar.

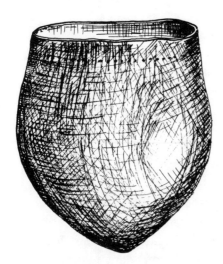

Algonkian jar.

Iroquois pot.

vessels for direct-fire cooking prior to the introduction of pottery.

Early clay vessels were crudely formed and tempered with vegetable fibers. A ball of clay was first pinched in the center, then worked with both hands to form a vessel. Or a flat clay pancake was molded over a gourd or stone. Eventually, coiling techniques were developed, and flat molded disks were built up with coils. Early Algonkian vessels were thick-walled, pointed at the base, and without decoration. It is believed the pointed, or conoidal base, was designed to allow maximum heat to surround the vessel while it was on the fire. Pots were supported in the fire by an arrangement of stones, or the pot was set in a depression in the center of the fire, where earth and embers could be packed up around it. As women improved their potting techniques, the walls of vessels became a little thinner and the base less pointed. Finer tempering materials, such as ground shell, were used in place of coarser tempering materials. Coils on these pots were kneaded together smoothly, and ridges were not evident in the exterior walls.

Algonkian pottery eventually became influenced by the Iroquois, who made pottery vessels with round bottoms and heavy collars on top. The Iroquois often made couble-necked bowls, with holes or lugs in the sides for carrying. The best-quality clay was tempered with finely ground quartz, flint, and ground mussel shells. A bark paddle was used to shape the pots. Sharp-edged mussel shells were used to shape the heavy collars. Collar designs on Iroquois pots often included sculptured animals or the faces of spirits. Background designs were in the form of crosses or stripes, incised in the clay with sharp animal bones or pointed wooden sticks.

Although coiled pots were common in the extreme eastern portion of the United States, tribes near the Great Lakes modeled pots by striking the outside of the clay with a wooden paddle while holding round stones or hard, round balls of clay

Coastal clay cliffs, Martha's Vineyard.

Surface clay in the Southwest.

inside the pots. Usually bowl-shaped, the pots were made in a variety of sizes. The Iroquois also favored the paddle-and-anvil technique—pressing coils together by paddling with a smooth bark paddle. Heavy sections of a paddled pot were scraped away with a sharp mussel shell.

How to Locate Clay

Native Americans had to locate, dig, and clean clay before it could be worked. It is quite possible to learn what the Indians knew about raw clay by emulating these early potters. To dig into the earth for materials and then to transform them into useful utensils can be an exciting and rewarding experience.

Clay is created by water and wind-blown sand wearing away rocks. Thus, there is abundant clay in the earth's crust. A sedimentary type of clay can be found between layers of sand and silt, along rivers and streams, in desert basins, on lake and ocean bottoms, and along coastal shores. Residual clay, found near the earth's surface, is formed by erosion over shallow-lying igneous rock. Although these clays are not always of good quality, they were often used by the Indians.

We normally think of clay as very fine soil, which it is. However, it is also a complex mixture of mineral substances. When mixed with water and heated, these substances become like metamorphosed rock, which is created by extreme heat, pressure or chemical changes in the earth's crust. The essential elements in clay are silica and alumina. Clay, when wet, is sticky and feels slippery, but it will hold a shape when dry.

The U.S. Geological Survey produces maps that show the earth's stratas; i.e., the layers of earth that pile on top of one another. With the help of these maps, you may be able to identify general areas of clay deposition. Topographical maps, also published by the U.S. Geological Survey, are more detailed. They cover specific areas, note locations of old mines, and indicate land contours, elevations, and stream locations. To obtain these maps, look in your telephone book under U.S. Government, Interior Department, or Geological Survey, for the addresses. Or, you can call or write your state agricultural extension service. They have information on all types of soils of each region and may be able to give you some general locations.

Because most clay deposits are covered by a layer of topsoil, the most convenient place to look for clay is near construction sites, where the topsoil has been removed and the substrata are exposed. Slow-moving streams are also good places, since the fine particles of clay are often deposited in layers along the banks.

To find out if a material is clay, wet a handful of it and rub it between your fingers. Try molding it to see if it will hold a shape. If it is sticky, it is probably clay. It is difficult to tell from the color of raw clay what the color will be after firing. As a general rule, grey clay fires to a red or buff color; red and yellow clay to a shade of red. Clay that is gray or black, due to organic matter, may fire white or red. Most raw clays contain iron-oxide impurities that prevent them from being fired at high temperatures. However, Indian pottery was always low-fired because temperatures never exceeded about 1700°F. in their open fires. An advantage to the iron oxides in raw clay is the beautiful orange-red colors obtained after firing.

A fine, pure clay, called kaolin, can be found in Alabama, Arkansas, Florida, Georgia, Idaho, Kansas, Mississippi, Montana, New Mexico, North and South Carolina, and Washington.

How to Clean and Prepare Clay

Materials

> Pail
> Shovel
> Clay
> Fine wire, approximately 24 inches
>   long
> Wood handles (optional)
> Hammer
> ⅛-inch wire screen (optional)
> Water
> Temper

1. Fill a pail with clay from a local clay deposit. At the site, remove as much of the large pebbles and other debris as possible.

How to clean and prepare clay.

2. Attach two wooden handles to each end of a length of wire. Form the clay into a ball and cut it in half with the wire. Pick out the pebbles, twigs, and grass exposed by the cut. Continue to cut the clay into one-inch slabs, cleaning out the debris as you cut. When the ball is completely cut, restack the clay and cut it again. Repeat this process at least ten times. The clay must be completely clean before it is kneaded. (The wire can also be streched tightly across two fixed points, freeing both hands.) Or, you can allow the clay to dry out completely and pound it into powder with a hammer or other heavy, blunt tool. Put the powdered clay through a fine ⅛-inch screen to eliminate debris. Add just enough water to the powdered clay so that it will hold its shape when formed into a ball.

4. Kneading is the most important step in clay preparation. Clay can be kneaded like bread, or it can be pounded. Place a lump of clay on a table and pound it with your fist into a flat pancake. Fold the pancake in half twice and pound it again. Repeat this procedure about eight times. Although it takes a great deal of time and a lot of hard work to knead clay, the more it is kneaded, the easier it will be to shape. Proper kneading eliminates air pockets and improves plas-

ticity, or moldability. Clay that is *short,* or non-plastic, will crack while it is being kneaded. Short clay, which contains more coarse material than fine, is difficult to work into pots, but it is worth trying. Clay that is extremely smooth, with no coarse material in it, is too plastic. Temper, or coarse material, must be added. Temper, in the form of ground shell, ground plant pots, or sand, can be added in small quantities to give the clay body and added strength.

How to Coil Pots

Materials

> Prepared clay
> Shallow bowl, 6 inches in diameter
> Damp cloth
> A piece of gourd, shell, or wood
> Anvil (a round object made of pottery
>   or stone)
> Paddle
> Water (optional)

1. Dig and clean the clay. Make four separate balls of it, each the size of a tennis ball. Wrap three of the balls in a damp cloth and put them aside.

2. Flatten the fourth clay ball with both hands, pressing it into a 6-inch disk. It should be approximately ¼ inch to ½ inch thick.

3. Set the disk inside a shallow bowl and turn up the edges of the disk *(A).* A wooden bowl or a broken pottery base makes a good support for the clay disk,

Setting a clay disk
inside a bowl.

A

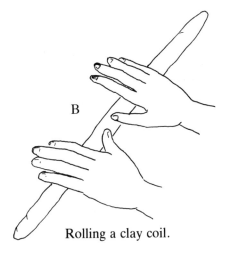

B

Rolling a clay coil.

C

Welding coils on the inside.

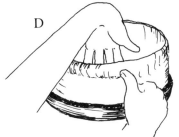

D

Welding coils on the outside.

E

Adding a new coil.

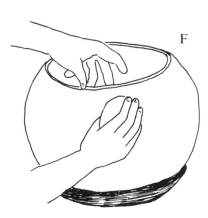

F

Shaping a pot with smooth stones.

G

Shaping with paddle and anvil.

since the clay can be easily removed from a porous base. Clay will stick to glazed dishes.

4. Unwrap another ball of clay and roll it out on a table into a long coil *(B)*. Use the palms of your hands and fingers to roll it back and forth. Roll evenly and slowly, working from the center outward. The coil should be 17 inches long and 1 inch in diameter in order to fit the 6-inch base.

5. Place the coil *inside* the upturned edge of the clay disk, wrapping it around the base *(C)*. If the coil is too long, pinch a piece off the end to make it fit. If it is too short, take it off and roll it some more.

6. Welding coils together is the most important aspect of pot building. Coils must be firmly welded together or they will separate when dry *(D)*. To weld coils on the *inside,* hold one hand against the outside wall and push the clay down with your thumb, being careful to push just the right amount to fill in the area between coil and base. To weld the coil to the base on the *outside,* hold one hand *inside* and pull the clay down on the *outside.*

7. Make another coil and place it on top of the first one. Be sure the *outside* of this coil lines up with the *outside* of the previous one *(E)*. Because the last coil was made thinner when it was welded to the base, it will be thinner than the coil being added. At least one third of the new coil should extend into the interior of the pot. This slight overhang helps to keep the walls of the pot vertical. Since traditional Indian shapes tend to go in at the rim, vertical walls are easier to shape inward. Don't try to shape the pot

while the coils are being welded. Shaping is done when the last coil is on. Indian potters often created different shapes by varying the diameter of the coils.

8. When the third coil is welded on, the pot may be smoothed and shaped. You can shape it with a piece of smooth shell, wood, or a piece of gourd. Or, you can use the paddle-and-anvil technique. To shape the wet pot with a piece of shell, gourd, or wood, hold one hand against the inside wall and work the smooth side of the scraper diagonally around the pot, turning it as you go. Gently push on the walls from the *inside* while smoothing the outside. The walls will crack if stretched too fast, so work slowly and keep turning. The walls of a three-coil pot will stretch to a diameter of 22 inches around the midsection, where the pot bulges, and will be about ¼ inch to ½ inch thick *(F)*.

9. Indian pots have extremely thin walls, an advantage handmade pottery has over wheel-thrown. Thin-walled pots are less likely to break in the fire, which may be why Indian potters worked them so thin. Natural materials, such as shell, stiff grass, or cords, can be pressed into the wet clay when it is smooth. Or you can use your fingernails. Southeastern tribes carved designs on wooden stamps and pressed them into the exterior walls.

10. The paddle-and-anvil technique is used to shape or smooth pots when wet. Build a coil pot, but instead of scraping and shaping, paddle the outside with a wooden paddle while holding an anvil against the interior wall *(G)*.

How to Model and Mold Pots

Materials

Prepared clay
Convex/concave mold
Wooden paddle (optional)
Anvil (optional)

MODELING

1. Model or pinch a large ball of clay about the size of an orange. Press a hole in the center of the clay and slowly enlarge it with both hands. Keep the thumbs inside while rotating the ball of clay. Gently squeeze and thin the walls between fingers and thumbs as the pot is turned. This takes practice, so don't be discouraged if the walls are uneven and thick at first *(A)*, *(B)*. Or, you can make a hole in the ball of clay and enlarge it with both hands until the center is big enough to insert an anvil. Hold the anvil inside the pot and paddle the outside wall directly against it, turning the pot as you paddle. The clay will stretch and the pot will become enlarged. This technique works well for small ports, but it is not practical for largers ones because the walls will not hold their shape if stretched too much *(C)*.

MOLDING

1. Flatten a clay ball into a large pancake about ½ inch thick. Mold the pancake over a bowl, large stone, shell, gourd, precut wooden mold, or other convex form. Molds can also be made in a concave base, such as inside a basket, a bowl, or a similar object *(D)*.

60

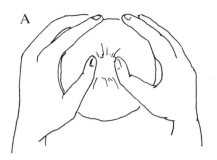

Pressing hole in a clay ball.

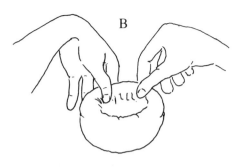

Rotating a clay ball while modeling.

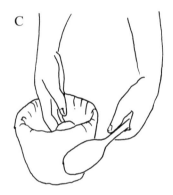

Modeling with paddle and anvil.

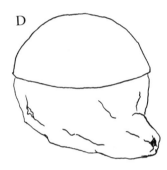

Molding a clay disk over a gourd.

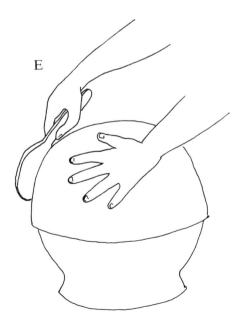

Molding and paddling clay over a convex base.

2. Allow the clay to become leather-hard, then remove it from the mold. Finish and decorate the pot by incising, slipping, polishing, or painting.

3. Molding and coiling are techniques that are often combined. Mold a 6-inch flat disk over a convex form, and add coils overlapping each one slightly on the outside. Beat downward with a paddle to bond the coils together *(E)*.

4. Allow the pot to dry leather-hard, then remove it from the mold. Finish and decorate the pot by incising, slipping, polishing, or painting it.

How to Finish and Decorate Pots

Materials

Water
Pail
Clay
1-inch brush
Bowl for slip
Smooth stone
Sharp bone or stick
Pigments
½-inch brush

SLIPPING

1. Slips are applied when the pot is leather-hard, which means that the pot is stiff enough to be handled without changing its shape. Gently squeeze the walls of the pot to test for stiffness.

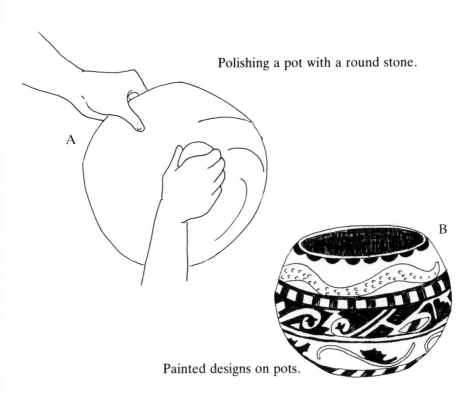

Polishing a pot with a round stone.

A

B

Painted designs on pots.

2. Mix any good-quality clay with water to the consistency of heavy cream and put it through a fine sieve to eliminate any impurities.

3. Brush on the slip with a 1-inch brush, using long, even strokes. Allow the slip to dry completely before a second coat is applied. Slips fill in small holes in the pot surface and give a smooth exterior to the pot for polishing and painting. Two coats of slip are enough to cover most imperfections.

POLISHING

1. Polish the pot with a smooth, round stone while it is leather-hard. Rub the stone in different directions, going over and over the same spot until it is shiny. Be patient. This takes a lot of time. The longer a pot is polished, the shinier it will be after firing *(A)*.

63

2. Designs can be incised or scratched on the polished pot with a sharp bone or stick. Don't allow the incisions to be deeper than ¹⁄₁₆ inch, otherwise the walls of the pot will be weakened.

Paint is made from diluted clays, or slips. The color of clay is affected by the amount of iron or metallic oxide in it. Therefore, to change the color of clay, oxides or pigments may be added. Pigments may be purchased at pottery supply houses. Pots may also be painted with poster paint *after* they are fired. Poster paint has an oil or gum base, both organic materials, that would burn away during firing. Therefore, be sure to apply these paints *after* the pot is fired. Use a ½-inch brush to paint on authentic designs *(B)*.

How to Direct-fire Pottery

Materials

	Shovel
20 to 30	round stones
	Twigs and kindling wood
15 to 20	two-foot logs
8 to 10	potsherds
	Prepared pots
	Matches
	08 cone (optional)

1. Dig a shallow pit, 4 feet in diameter, away from trees or brush. Be sure the ground and wood is dry or you will "create" steam around your pots. Also, make sure that the pots are thoroughly dry before firing. Even after pots have dried in the sun, small amounts of water may remain in the clay. New England tribes

Setting pots over twigs.

Covering pots with potsherds.

Placing logs on a fire.

Firing pots.

Removing pots from a fire.

Coiled, modeled, and molded pots.

often "burned" away excess moisture by placing the pots near the cooking fire for several days. If moisture is left in the clay when it is fired, steam will build up inside and the pot will explode.

2. Line the pit with 20 to 30 round stones. Place a layer of twigs or kindling on the stones and cover with half of the logs and more twigs.

3. Invert the pots over the twigs. If you have a clay cone to test for temperature, put it in with the pots *(A)*.

4. Place the potsherds on top of the pots to hold them in the heat and keep the temperature even *(B)*. Put the remaining logs on top of the potsherds *(C)*.

5. Light the bottom layer of kindling and allow the fire to build up slowly until water-smoking is complete *(D)*. Temperatures cannot be controlled in direct-fire pits because so much heat is lost by radiation and because there are no draft controls. You will have to experiment. The fire should be kept going for at least two or three hours. Clay will harden and no longer disintegrate in water if fired to a temperature of 1700°F. For clay to melt and fuse together like glass, temperatures must reach about 2000°F. An 08 clay cone bends at 1700°F. If you used a cone and it is bent, you will know the pot is fired hard.

6. Leave the pots in the fire until they have cooled enough to be removed with your bare hands. If no cone was used to test the temperature, set a cooled pot in a pail of water. It will return to clay if it was not properly fired *(E)*, *(F)*.

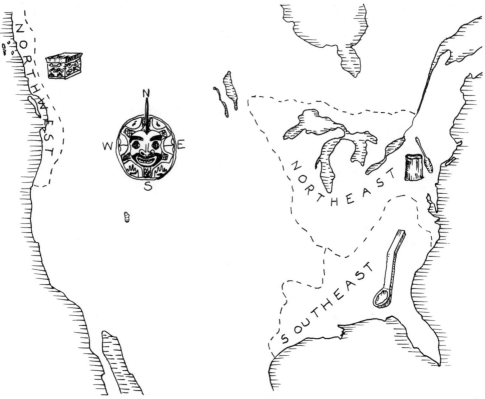

Map of woodenware regions.

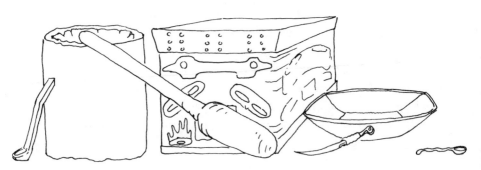

Woodenware in group.

Woodworking tools.

3

WOODENWARE

Woodworking Tools

Woodworking tools, used by Native Americans, were limited by today's standards. However, huge trees were felled by burning and scraping, and utensils of all shapes and sizes were made with bone, stone, and shell tools. Stone adzes, chisels, knives, scrapers, and mauls, as well as wooden wedges, were standard tools of the woodworker. In the Northwest, the most valuable woodworking tools were stone adzes, with handles made of hardwood and blades made of shell or stone. The cutting blade was at a right angle to the handle.

In the Northeast and Southeast, a curved or crooked knife

was the most useful carving tool. This knife had a blade that was curved on one side and relatively straight on the other. Adz and knife blades were replaced with iron after the arrival of the Europeans. Bowls and dishes were often burned, scraped with an adz, and then finished with a curved or crooked knife. Woodworkers in the Northeast also used bark to fashion utensils. With the exception of sharp cutting stones and awls, bark required few tools to work.

Northwest

On the Northwest coast, spruce and fir forests sprung up in the barren soils left by retreating glaciers. Hemlock and cedar followed. Cottonwood, willow, and alder trees eventually took their places beside rivers and streams throughout the region. Indian tribes who lived in the shadows of forested fjords, on narrow strips of land along the coast, took advantage of the region's most important natural resource—wood. The tough, cross-fibered wood of the spruce, fir, and hemlock did not yield to stone tools. But alder and red and yellow cedar, yielded and favored woodworking.

Tribes of the Northwest were expert fishermen as well as skilled woodworkers. Utensils were created to meet the needs of an active and productive fishing industry. Dishes, trays, spoons, ladles, and ceremonial and storage vessels were carved out of cedar and alder. Like many other tribes of North America, burning and scraping was the chief technique for felling trees. The trees were first packed around the base with wet moss, then burned and scraped below the packing. Wet moss kept the fire from spreading up the tree. The stone adz (later replaced with the iron ax) was used to remove charred wood.

Very fine, sharp jade knives were originally used to carve cedar. Hardwood, such as maple, was used where strength was

Interior of a Northwest Coast plank house.

essential. The wood could be worked with shell or beaver incisors—tools that were too blunt for conifer wood. Alder logs, used for dishes and trays, were burned and scraped. Alder was preferred for dishes because it did not impart flavors to food. Everyday dishes were undecorated and rectangular, with rounded ends and wide lips. Ceremonial dishes and bowls were decorated with stylistic designs, carved on the lips and exteriors. The Haida and Tsimshian carved bear, whale, beaver, and hawk motifs on ceremonial oil bowls.

Sewed or pegged cedar boxes, unique to the Northwest, were intricately kerfed, which means that a channel or cut was made in the wood. The kerfing was done where the board was

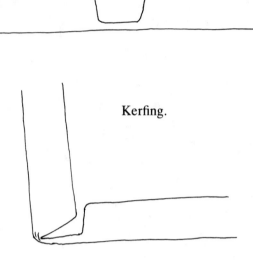

Kerfing.

to bend. The technique of heating and bending wood was highly developed in the Northwest. Cedar logs were split into boards by driving wedges along the grain of the log with a mallet. The wedges came in a variety of tapers, depending on how one wanted to control the direction of cleavage. Boards about one inch thick were cut for boxes, and the corners were kerfed to form precise right angles. The kerfed area was steamed by placing hot seaweed over the kerf or by holding the board over a fire smothered with wet seaweed. This process was used to bend each kerfed joint until the board bent to form a square. Joints were sewed or pegged together. Small holes were drilled in the wood with a small drill mounted in a straight shaft and rotated between the palms. Spruce-root twigs or wooden pegs were placed in the holes. The bottom of a box was made by cutting a board to exact measurements and joining it by sewing or pegging. All the boxes were highly sanded with dogfish skin or rushes. The boxes were used for storing water and for cooking by stone-boiling. Fresh water and supplies of fish oil were also stored in boxes during voyages at sea.

72

Southeast

Although the climate of the Southeast does not favor the preservation of wooden artifacts, archeologists have evidence that woodworking once flourished in the region. Wooden utensils, carved animals, masks, and figures, attributed to the Calusa Indians of southern Florida, were unearthed early in this century. These artifacts were beautifully carved and elaborately inlaid with shell.

Bald cypress—a soft, fine-grained wood—was used by tribes of the Southeast for many years. Cypress groves once lined the Gulf and Florida coasts and also flourished inland in lowlands, where their roots remained underwater most of the year. Cypress trees do not have the hollow trunks or stems that are characteristic of other water-loving plants.

Lowland soil is so saturated with water that very little oxygen gets to the roots that need oxygen to survive. To compensate for this, cypress trees develop roots aboveground. The roots, called knees, grow around the base of the tree and are hollow. Southeastern Indians removed the knee portion of a root to make bowls.

Tribes of the Southeast were primarily farmers. Their productive vegetable gardens amazed European explorers because the only farm implement of the Indians was a single-blade hoe. Fortunately, rich hammocks of soil in the swamps and prairies of Florida, and fertile levee ridges inland, were free of rocks or gravel and, therefore, easy to work.

Wooden mortars and pestles, made from hickory or beech logs, were essential for grinding corn. Mud or wet seaweed was packed around the outside edge of a log and the center was burned and scraped. Pestles were heavy on the bottoms and tapered toward the tops. Corn was soaked overnight in wood ash and water, which produced a lye that helped remove the corn hulls. Then the corn was ground and winnowed in a

This Cherokee woman is using a wooden mortar and pestle. *(Smithsonian Institution National Anthropological Archives)*

Sofkee spoon.

Grinding koonti in mortar.

Zula Stevens works on a carved wooden bowl. *(U.S. Department of the Interior, Indian Arts and Crafts Board)*

flat basket until the grain separated from the hull. The cracked corn was made into soup, called *sofkee* by the Creek Indians. Other tribes called it *hominy*. Corn kernels were pounded very fine for flour. Cooking was done in larger pottery vessels, later replaced by iron. A large sofkee spoon was used to transfer food from the pot to individual dishes or the spoon was passed around.

Besides farming, the Seminole of Florida dug large quantities of koonti roots, which they washed to remove bitter properties. The roots were placed in piles next to a long pine log that had several mortars about nine inches deep. Each mortar had a pestle. Women and children pounded the koonti roots into pulp. The pulp was then taken to a creek, water was added, and it was set aside for several hours. Then it was strained, and the starchy sediment in the water was left to ferment. After several days, the fermented flour was spread on palmetto leaves to dry before it was used to make koonti bread.

The Seminole Indians continued to make spoons, ladles, mortars, and pestles well into the twentieth century. Less than twenty years ago, wood carving was revived in the Choctaw and Cherokee reservations, using new tools and techniques. Graceful bowls and trays, with traditional designs and shapes, are still being produced today by residents of both reservations.

Northeast

The Indians of the Northeast are often referred to as "the forest dwellers." Towering stands of spruce and fir, interspersed with beech, maple, and birch, once dominated the landscape. The woodlands were a mixed blessing for the Indians. While the trees were an important source of natural material, working the hardwoods into tools and utensils and

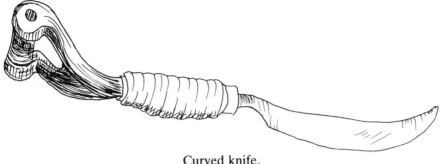

Curved knife.

wrestling trees from the rocky soil to plant crops was an arduous task.

Eastern Algonkian tribes lived in small settlements along the Eastern seaboard where they fished, hunted, and farmed. Central Algonkian tribes harvested native wild rice from the marshes of rivers and lakes. Like corn, rice was preserved for winter. The Iroquois lived in the fertile valleys south of the Great Lakes. They were large-scale farmers, who worked wood with stone tools. Trees were felled by burning and chipping with a stone adz. Stone blades were also used for gouging, chiseling, and scraping wood. Wooden wedges were used to split logs. Curved iron knives eventually replaced the stone blades.

Cooking was generally done in pottery vessels by the Eastern Algonkian and Iroquois, while birch bark was used by the Central Algonkian. All tribes preferred wood or bark utensils for serving and eating food. Bowls and dishes were made from tree burls or logs. Tree burls—round, large lumps—are created by rapid growth in one specific area on a tree, usually on the trunk.

European merchants traded iron with Northeastern tribes for fur. By the early seventeenth century, the iron knife had replaced most stone tools. Some Indian woodworkers felt the stone knife produced the best curved lines, while the European iron knife made straight lines and sharp angles in wood.

The Iroquois pounded corn with a wooden mortar and pestle.
(Smithsonian Institution National Anthropological Archives)

The most essential wooden utensils were the mortar and pestle. Without these, a woman could not prepare corn. A mortar was made by charring a deep hole in one end of a two-foot pine log. The log was set on the ground, and the upturned side was packed with mud, around the outer edge of the log. A fire, set in the center of the log, was allowed to burn for several hours. When the fire burned out, the charred area was scraped, and a new fire was started. This process continued until the mortar was deep enough to keep the corn from flying out when being ground.

Standard utensils in every home included spoons, ladles, bowls, dishes, and trays; many tribes often had individual dishes, cups, and spoons. Beech, basswood, and maple were preferred for bowls, while birchwood was used for spoons and ladles. Cherry, ash, horse chestnut, and maple were used to make spoons and ladles. Spoon and ladle handles were carved so that the handle end curved over the edge of the pot or bowl to keep it from slipping into the food. Popular handle designs include ducks, swans, pigeons, bears, and dogs. Very elaborate designs, sometimes inlaid with shell, adorned ceremonial ladles. The Iroquois often decorated their wooden utensils with human and wild animal figures.

Indians who lived between Newfoundland and Alaska, near the Great Lakes, and as far southeast as Long Island, used bark from the paper birch for most of their household utensils. While bark is generally considered to be a different material than wood, it is included in the craft of woodworking. Indians of the Northeast used both the inner and outer bark of birch trees for making a variety of utensils. Seamless, green bark containers, filled with water, could be placed directly over a fire for cooking, but they could only be used once before they were charred. However, the same containers could be used many times for the stone-boiling method of cooking. Birch bark is easy to work and durable. It does not impart a taste to food or water and helps prevent food decay when used for

Algonkian wooden spoon.

Algonkian wooden tray.

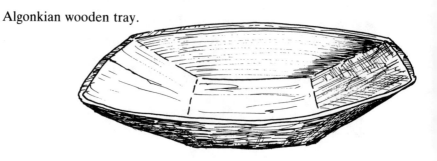

Carved bowls and cups. *(Idaho Historical Society)*

storage. Bark vessels were also used to collect and winnow wild rice; shallow bark dishes, with sloping sides, were often used for eating. Pails and buckets, large enough to hold three gallons, were made out of a single rectangular strip of bark, shaped by heating, bending, and folding. Twigs or spruce roots were used to fasten the ends of the bark together.

Maple sugaring was an important activity for the Algonkian, who used bark containers of all sizes in the sugaring process. Large, seamless containers were used to collect and boil maple sap. A cone-shaped bark mold was used to hold maple syrup until it hardened, and the filled cones were taken on hunting trips in winter. Passamaquoddy Indians made blueberry pre-

Algonkian maple-sugaring scene.

Chippewa woman removing bark from tree. *(Smithsonian Institution National Anthropological Archives)*

serves by spreading sheets of birch bark with boiled berries and drying them in the sun. The sheets were then rolled up with the berries in them and stored. Vessels, used for purposes other than cooking or storing water, were made by cutting and sewing. Box-shaped bark storage bins, with covers, were used to store wild rice. These boxes had hardwood rims, sewn with basswood fibers or spruce roots. Great Lakes tribes, who continued to make bark containers during the nineteenth century, were reluctant to give them up because bark was easy to obtain and to work. It also cost them nothing.

South of the Great Lakes, where birch trees are less prevalent, the bark of elm, hickory, and oak was used to make household utensils. Elm bark, which is heavy and rough-textured, was fashioned into trays by removing the outer bark from the edge and sides of a bark strip, then folding the peeled portion upward. Very large containers were reinforced with willow or ash splints, laced on with spruce roots. Holes or cracks were mended with black spruce resin, collected by making a small slash on a black spruce. The cut was left open for a year or more before the hardened sap was collected by whittling it into a soft bag. When the resin was placed in boiling water, the melted pitch floated to the top.

Bark was stripped from live trees in the early spring. The cambrium layer of cells lies between the sapwood and inner bark. It is in the process of cell division during the spring, when bark can be easily removed. The cambrium layer increases the girth of a tree by adding new cells to both the sapwood and inner bark each year.

Woodworking Materials

EASTERN WHITE PINE *(Pinus strobus)*

Eastern white pine—also called sapling, pumpkin, soft or Weymouth pine—once grew in almost pure stands. It flourishes from Newfoundland to Manitoba, in northeastern Iowa, Wisconsin, Michigan, New England, and Pennsylvania. It also grows in the Appalachian Mountains and northern Georgia. These pine trees, the largest in the East, grow under almost any climatic condition if they have adequate moisture. They are usually found in the company of hemlocks, red pines, and a variety of hardwoods. They can be distinguished by their

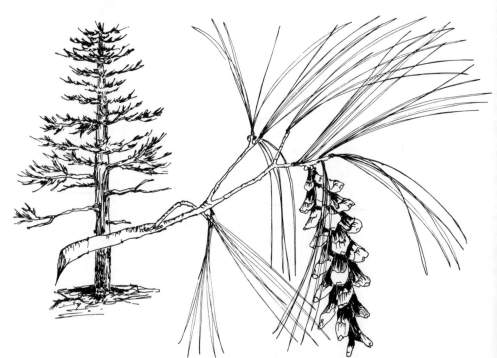

Eastern white pine.

horizontally spreading limbs and blue-green crowns. Leaves of the Eastern white pine grow in blue-green bunches of five; each is three to five inches long. Tiny, upright green cones appear on the end of twigs, just behind new leaves. The cones turn down the second year and grow to four to six inches long. The cones open during the fall of their second year, allowing winged seeds to be dispersed by the wind. The bark of the tree is characterized by long, broad, dark-gray ridges. The wood is soft, creamy white to reddish-brown, and straight-grained. Indians of the Northeast made large dugout canoes and corn-grinding mortars out of pine. Colonial settlers used the pinewood to build their homes and furniture. The British Navy made their masts out of pine trunks during the Revolutionary War. But the lightness and strength that make the wood so useful also led to its demise. Oxen and horse teams hauled huge quantities of trees on sleds over the snows to rivers, where they were floated to market. By 1900, the only virgin stands of Eastern white pine were in the southern Appalachian Mountains.

PAPER BIRCH *(Betula papyrifera)*

Paper birch—often called canoe, silver, or white birch—is the most widely distributed of all the world's birches. The trees are found from Newfoundland to Alaska, south to Pennsylvania and Long Island, around the Great Lakes, and west to Iowa and Minnesota.

Paper birch trees prefer rich, moist, sandy soils, commonly found near water. They grow in company with white pine, red pine, red spruce, aspen, and yellow birch. Paper birch has replaced both white pine and spruce on cut or burned-over land in Canada, Michigan, and New England. The tree grows from 60 to 80 feet high in dense forests, but is a mere shrub in the northern Appalachian mountains.

Mature paper birch trees have round crowns and long

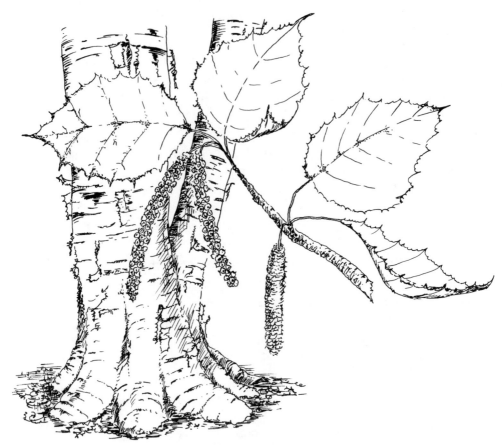

Paper birch.

trunks. Their thick leaves are double-toothed and oval—two
to three inches long, and two inches wide. They are light green
on top and yellow-green underneath. Male flowers are in the
form of pendulous brown catkins, while female flowers are
greenish, slender, and erect. Birch fruit is cone-shaped—
nutlets with long, broad wings.

The main feature of the paper birch tree is its bark, which is
creamy white or bronze and marked with raised lenticels, or
breathing pores. The bark can easily be removed from young

trees and older branches. It peels into thin papery layers. The inner bark is bright orange. The bark should be taken from freshly cut logs because bark taken from a live tree will kill the plant. Tribes of the North used the bark of paper birch for canoes, rainwear, moose calls, mats, trays, dishes, pails, and covers for their wigwams. The Indians used the hard, close-grained wood for canoe paddles and snowshoe frames. Today, paper birch wood is used in the manufacture of wooden toys, spools, clothespins, toothpicks, dowels, shoe pegs, and shoe lasts.

WESTERN RED CEDAR *(Thuja plicata)*

One of the largest trees of the Northwest coastal area, western red cedar—often called canoe cedar, Pacific red cedar, or Shinglewood—was an important source of natural material for weaving and woodworking for Indians of the

Western red cedar.

region. The knot-free cedar trees often grew to a height of two hundred feet along the rainy, humid coastline. The trees, found with Douglas fir and western hemlocks, are cone-shaped. Their young branches reach upward, while their mature branches turn gracefully downward. The leaves are small and scalelike, forming lacy sprays that emit a lovely fragrance. Each cone, which is one-half inch long, drops double-winged cone seeds during autumn. The empty cones turn upward and remain on the tree until the following summer.

The wood is reddish-brown when freshly cut and very aromatic. The bark is fibrous, stringy, and tough enough to be peeled from young trees in twenty- to thirty-foot strips. It was used by tribes of the Northwest for rope, matting, napkins, baskets, and clothing. The soft-to-medium grained wood is free of pitch. Because it splits and carves easily, it was used to make dugout canoes, totem poles, house planks, and wooden utensils. The tree is still an important source of building material because it resists decay and insects.

How to Burn and Scrape a Mortar and Grind Corn

Materials

A pine log, 24 inches long and about
    14 inches in diameter
Fine soil
Water
Twigs
10 to 20   charcoal briquettes
Matches
A sharp stone or clam shell

Charcoal burning in a pine mortar.

Grinding corn in a mortar
with a very old stone pestle.

A heavy tree branch or long, narrow
stone (for pestle)
Corn (any variety)

1. Set the log on end in an open area. Mix the soil and water to a thick mud. If it is too wet, it will run into the area you want to burn.

2. Pack the mud around the edge of the log, leaving the center free for burning and scraping.

3. Pile twigs in the opening and light them. When they are burning briskly, place a few pieces of charcoal on top. You may have to blow on the fire to get the charcoal going *(A)*.

4. When the charcoal has burned out, scrape and chip away at the charred wood with a sharp stone or a clam shell.

5. Repeat the burning and chipping process until the hole is at least halfway down the log. If the hole is not deep enough, the corn will fly out during the grinding.

6. Make a pestle out of a heavy branch or locate a long, narrow stone. Put a small quantity of corn in the mortar and grind to a fine powder *(B)*.

How to Make Birch Bark Containers

Materials

Birch bark, 15 inches by 12 inches
Birch bark, 12 inches in diameter
3 to 4 yards of natural bark cordage or twine
Sharp knife
Pan of hot water
awl

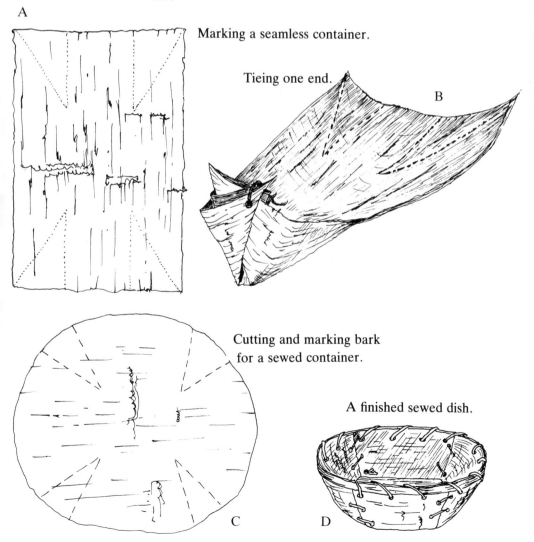

A

Marking a seamless container.

Tieing one end.

B

Cutting and marking bark
for a sewed container.

A finished sewed dish.

C   D

Seamless birch bark container.

1. Seamless containers do not need to be accurately measured. On the 15-by-12 inch piece of bark, draw a line about 4 inches long from each corner toward the center, then from the end of this line back to the outside edge *(A)*.

2. Hold the bark over a pan of steaming water. Allow the steam to soften each end of the bark at a time. Press folds into the V-angles with the outer bark on the outside of the container. Punch two small holes in the bark with an awl. Insert a piece of twine and tie it tightly *(B)*.

3. Repeat the same procedure for the other side. The finished container will be waterproof.

Note: Bark containers may also be cut and sewed. Cut gores in the 12-inch-round piece of bark and punch three holes with an awl along each side of the gore *(C)*. Lap one side over another and sew them together with natural cordage or twine. The finished container may be rimmed with a flexible wood strip, which can be sewed on with natural cordage *(D)*.

How to Make Bark Cordage

Materials

	Sharp knife
	Basswood bark
	Large container of water
2 to 3	rocks (for weight)
	Pan of boiling water

1. Cut the bark of a young basswood tree in the spring.

Stripping bark from a basswood tree.

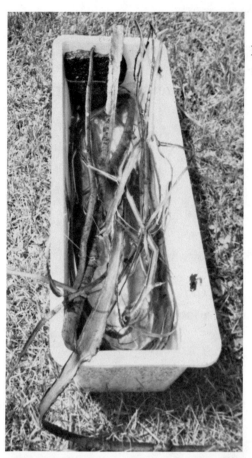

Basswood bark
soaking in water.

Stripping away the
inner fibers of basswood.

Do not hesitate to cut deeply because basswood bark is very thick even in young saplings. Make a slash up the tree in a straight line. Cut around the base of the tree in a circle.

2. Gently pull the bark upward. It will peel off quite easily.

3. Place the bark in a pond or stream, or in a large container of water. Weigh down the bark with stones. Allow the bark to soak for at least a week. (A short-cut method of removing the inner bark is to boil it in water for several hours.)

4. Peel away the soft inner fibers, drape them over your knee, and roll them back and forth. Twist them together as you roll. This cordage may be used for weaving mats, twining baskets, or for sewing.

How to Carve a Spoon

Materials

2	gouges, curvature #5, ⅜ inch width
	curvature #6, ⅝ inch width
	Wooden mallet
	Metal vise
2-by-4-inch	block of wood
	A sturdy table
2	C-clamps
2	pieces of scrap lumber
10-by-3-inch	piece of wood, approximately 1 inch thick

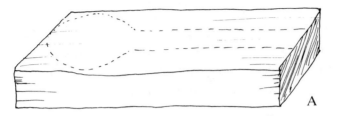

Sketch spoon outline.

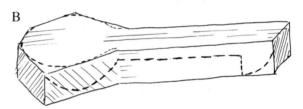

Rough-cut of a spoon.

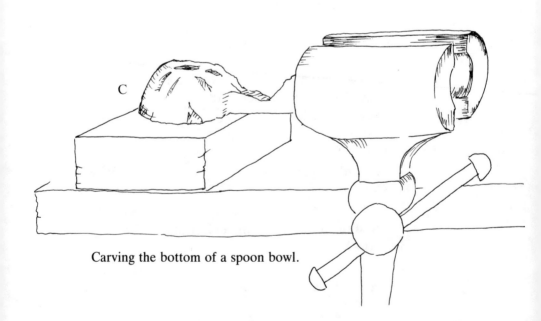

Carving the bottom of a spoon bowl.

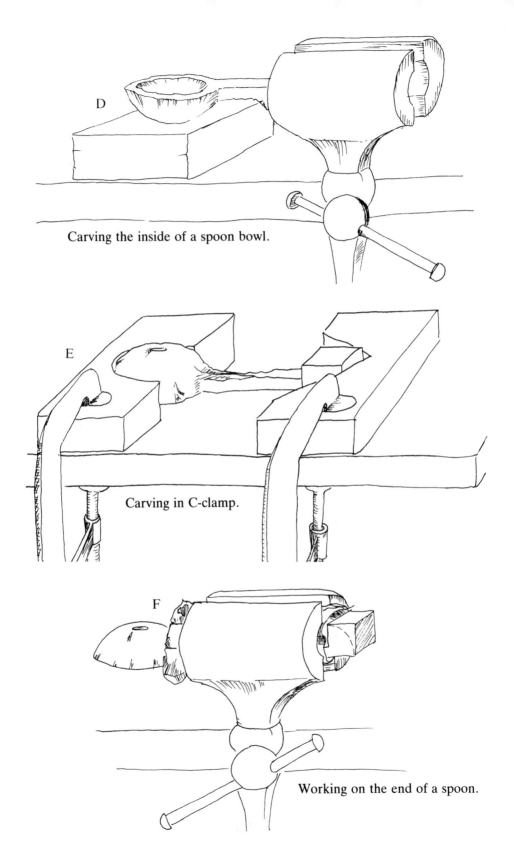

D

Carving the inside of a spoon bowl.

E

Carving in C-clamp.

F

Working on the end of a spoon.

Handsaw
Sandpaper
Clear polyurethane varnish
Small paint brush
Rasp (optional)

1. Cut a 10-by-3-inch piece of wood, about 1 inch thick, from a fireplace log.

2. Draw a rough outline of a spoon on the top, flat portion of the wood *(A)*.

3. Cut out along the outline with a handsaw, and draw a rough outline of the spoon on the side of the wood *(B)*.

4. Place the rough-cut spoon in a vise and carve the bottom of the spoon bowl with a #5 gouge and a wooden mallet. It is not wise to carve toward a metal vise because the gouge will be permanently damaged if it slips and hits the metal. Therefore, place a large block of wood under the spoon bowl, some distance from the vise, and clamp only the spoon handle in the vise. Remember to carve with the grain as much as possible and to carve only small pieces out of the bowl so the wood will not splinter. Work from the center outward, and keep both hands on the tools at all times. You may also shape the back of the bowl with a rasp, which is easy to control *(C)*.

5. When the back of the spoon is roughly shaped, turn the spoon over and carve the inside of the bowl. As the bowl deepens, you will have to use the narrower, #6 gouge. Leave a wide rim on the bowl of the spoon at first. This can be trimmed during the finishing process *(D)*.

6. Because the handle cannot be worked on the vise, take the two pieces of scrap lumber and attach them to the table with C-clamps *(E)*. These will hold the spoon firmly while you carve the handle. The handle can be carved to almost any desired shape and thickness, but leave a 1-inch chunk of wood at the end. Don't carve the handle too thin; a thick handle makes the spoon sturdier. The end of the handle will be carved later to fit over the end of a bowl or pot.

7. Wrap the handle in several layers of rags or paper towels and clamp it in the vise so that the end piece can be carved or rasped *(F)*.

8. Put the spoon back in the C-clamp form to finish all carving, shaping, and smoothing.

9. Sand the entire spoon all over with coarse, then fine sandpaper. Give the spoon several coats of clear polyurethane varnish.

Finishing a carved spoon.

SELECTED BIBLIOGRAPHY

Butler,, Eva L., and Hadlock, Wendell S. *Uses of Birch-Bark in the Northeast.* The Robert Abbe Museum, Bar Harbor, Maine, Bulletin VII, 1957.

Burt, Jesse, and Ferguson, Robert B. *Indians of the Southeast: Then and Now.* New York: Abingdon Press, 1973.

Boas, Franz. "Methods in Indian Woodwork-Illustrated." *The Red Man,* Vol. 2, No. 8 (April 1910), pp. 2–10.

Collingwood, G.H., and Brush, Warren D. *Knowing Your Trees.* Washington, D.C.: The American Forestry Association, 1964.

Dockstader, Frederick. *Naked Clay: Unadorned Pottery of the American Indian.* New York: Museum of the American Indian, 1972.

Douglas, Frederick H., and D'Harnoncourt, René. *Indian Art of the United States*. New York: Arno Press, 1969.

Drucker, Philip. *Cultures of the Pacific Northwest*. Scranton, Pa.: Chandler Publishing Co., 1965.

Fenstermaker, Gerald B. "Iroquois Pottery." *Pennsylvania Archaeologist*. Vol. VI, No. 4 (January 1937).

Frances, Paul. *Spruce Root Basketry of the Alaska Tlingit*. Washington, D.C.: U.S. Department of the Interior, Bureau of Indian Affairs, 1944.

Harlow, William M., Ph.D. *Inside Wood*. Washington, D.C.: The American Forestry Association, 1970.

Heizer, Robert F. *Handbook of North American Indians*. Vol. 8. Washington, D.C.: Smithsonian Institution, 1978.

Hudson, Charles M. *The Southeastern Indians*. Knoxville, Tenn.: The University of Tennessee Press, 1976.

James, George Wharton. *Indian Basketry*. New York: Dover Publications, 1972.

Lismer, Marjorie. *Seneca Splint Basketry*. Washington, D.C.: United States Department of the Interior, Branch of Education, 1941.

Lyford, Carrie A. *Chippewa Crafts*. Washington, D.C.: United States Department of the Interior, Branch of Education, 1945.

Mason, Otis T. *Aboriginal American Basketry*. Salt Lake City, Utah: Peregrine Smith, Inc., 1976.

Newman, Sandra Corrie. *Indian Basket Weaving: How to Weave Pomo, Yurok, Pima and Navajo Baskets*. Flagstaff, Ariz.: Northland Press, 1974.

Palmer, E. Lawrence. *Fieldbook of Natural History*. New York: McGraw-Hill Book Company, 1949.

Peattie, Donald Culross. *A Natural History of Trees of Eastern and Central North America*. New York: Bonanza Books, 1948.

Schoewe, Charles G. "Uses of Wood and Bark Among the

Wisconsin Indians." *Wisconsin Archeologist.* Vol. 11, No. 4, 1932, pp. 148–52

Shepard, Anna O. *Ceramics for the Archaeologist.* Washington, D.C.: Carnegie Institution, 1956.

Speck, Frank G. *Montagnais Art in Birch-Bark, A Circumpolar Trait.* New York: Museum of the American Indian, 1937.

Whiteford, Andrew Hunter. *North American Indian Arts.* New York: Golden Press, 1973.

Willoughby, Charles. C. "Textile Fabrics of the New England Indians." *American Anthropologist.* Vol. 7, No. 1, Jan.–March 1905, pp. 85–93.

———. "Wooden Bowls of the Algonquian Indians." *American Anthropologist.* Vol. 10, No. 3, July–Sept. 1908, p. 423–34.

———. "Basketry." *Science N. S..* Vol. XVI, No. 392, July 4, 1902.

Wormington, H. M. *The Story of Pueblo Pottery.* Denver, Colo.: Denver Museum of Natural History. Museum Pictorial, No. 2, 1974.

COMMON METRIC EQUIVALENTS AND CONVERSIONS

Approximate

1 inch	= 25 millimeters
1 foot	= 0.3 meter
1 yard	= 0.9 meter
1 square inch	= 6.5 square centimeters
1 square foot	= 0.09 square meter
1 square yard	= 0.8 square meter
1 millimeter	= 0.04 inch
1 meter	= 3.3 feet
1 meter	= 1.1 yards
1 square centimeter	= 0.16 square inch

Accurate to Parts Per Million

inches × 25.4°	= millimeters
feet × 0.3048°	= meters
yards × 0.9144°	= meters
square inches × 6.4516°	= square centimeters
square feet × 0.092903	= square meters
square yards × 0.836127	= square meters

INDEX